Richard Davis is principal flute of the BBC Philharmonic, and also Senior Lecturer and an orchestral coach in the Royal Northern College of Music. He was the youngest section principal ever to be appointed. He has played in virtually all the major orchestras in Britain in his time, and he is active as a conductor, too. A number of composers have written flute works specially for him, including Sir Peter Maxwell Davies with his *Temenos with Mermaids and Angels*. After twenty years' playing as principal, he has decided that he would like to pass on his knowledge and experience of the profession to a new generation of performers, together with many secrets he has learnt in his career in performing.

D1117934

Becoming an Orchestral Musician

A GUIDE FOR ASPIRING PROFESSIONALS

by

Richard Davis

dlm

First published in 2004
by Giles de la Mare Publishers Limited
53 Dartmouth Park Hill, London NW5 1JD

Typeset by Tom Knott
Printed in China
through Colorcraft Ltd, Hong Kong
All rights reserved

A CIP record of this book is available
from the British Library

ISBN 1–900357–23–2 paperback original

For Linda, Bryden and Jonathan

'God gave us music so that we can pray without words.'
St Augustine, 354–430

Preface

Richard Davis's pioneering book is to be welcomed by orchestral players, prospective orchestral musicians, conductors, composers, senior management and their junior staff – and by anybody interested in the internal workings of a symphony orchestra.

Hitherto, there has been nothing comparable to help a student of college or pre-college age decide upon an orchestral career, nor to guide parents and teachers about its perils and pleasures. Here there are helpful guidelines concerning all the essential topics, including how to cope with nerves, intonation and counting difficulties, conductor problems, and strategies for survival in everyday orchestral circumstances. The mechanics of the orchestra are laid bare through interviews with orchestral principals and rank and file players, soloists, academics, music critics, fixers, chamber musicians and management.

There are probably more orchestras, amateur and professional, in Britain than ever before, and, with a new recognition of the importance of music in schools, this book will provide invaluable insights into one of the most rewarding musical professions.

Richard Davis has twenty years' experience as principal flute, and I have had the privilege of benefiting from his excellent musicianship and support as both composer and conductor with the BBC Philharmonic. He is also Senior Lecturer and an orchestral coach at the Royal Northern College of Music.

His timely book fills a gap in the literature with a lightness of touch and humour, and many a telling anecdote along the way, yet with a seriousness that is both profound and exactly to the point.

SIR PETER MAXWELL DAVIES
Master of the Queen's Music
Sanday, Orkney
26th July 2004

Contents

'When music sounds, all that I was I am
Ere to this haunt of brooding dust I came ...'
Walter de la Mare, poet, 1873–1956

Prologue

In 1979 a young musician was faced with a dilemma. Up to that point, his music-making had gone remarkably well – he had attained his grade eight with distinction after only two years and was a principal player in his county youth orchestra. Then an event made him come to doubt everything he had done. He had entered a major music competition. After passing through the early rounds with ease, he had reached the quarterfinals; and it was then that a panellist did an unusual thing. He handed the boy a note. It read: 'For your career's sake, stay behind for a chat.' After a three-hour wait, the distinguished musician and the boy met up and walked to a local café.

His opening remark was direct: 'You haven't won the round – you *do* know that don't you?' When the boy's heart had begun to beat again, they discussed what was wrong. The boy was indeed talented, he was told, and he did have a future. But major flaws in his playing were holding him back and needed to be addressed soon. His whole style was considered to be 'out of vogue'.

The panellist's motives were in fact well intentioned and he made it clear that poaching wasn't an issue when he said: 'Well, I'm not going to teach you.' Instead, he scribbled down some tone exercises on a paper napkin, and recommended a completely new direction for his studies. He then left the boy to ponder these words. 'A true talent, such as yours, will always succeed in getting a job; but with proper guidance that job will find you.'

The sixteen-year-old went home that night, his mind brimming with confusion. He just didn't know what to do, nor did his parents, and they asked themselves who this man was to give such advice, anyway? If only a book like this had been available to guide them.

A decision was taken and that boy, now a man, never looked back. During the following four years he won first prize in an international music competition, received glowing reviews from national newspapers for his London début and found himself sitting in the principal chair of a professional British symphony orchestra. Remarkably, the panellist's prophecy did come true as that particular job found him – but that's another story. There isn't a day that passes when the author of this book fails to wonder what would have happened to him if he had ignored the advice he was given in the café and had not changed his school of playing.

That there are opposing 'schools of thought' in music may surprise the reader. Surely beautiful, deeply felt playing that establishes a link between performer, composer and audience is *everyone's* goal. However, style is fluid: the art of playing is never to set your ideals in concrete but to evolve.

Foreword

'We shall never become musicians unless we understand the ideals of
temperance, fortitude, liberality and magnificence.'
Plato, 428/7–348/7 BC, from *The Republic*

The word 'orchestra' is derived from the Greek word meaning 'to
dance' and in the Roman theatre it referred to the area in front of
the stage where senators and dignitaries sat. Every day we hear the
word 'orchestrate' being used figuratively in business, politics and
sport, and yet few people know what it is like to play in that well-
orchestrated body of musicians known as a 'symphony orchestra'.
Little is understood about these highly motivated and disciplined
teams where each player plays an integral part and is acutely
aware of and reliant on every other player. Orchestral musicians
have to be able to switch instantly between supporting, following and leading. But how do so many individuals perform complex music on instruments that take a lifetime to master, in
complete synchronization? When you listen to an orchestra, you
are experiencing a process in which each player is continuously
making millions of adjustments aurally, visually, emotionally and
physically, and combining their collective talents into one organism. They perform concerts with apparent ease balancing their
levels of pressure, fusing their discipline and talent, and sur-
mounting exceptional obstacles. As you become aware of these
innate abilities, your senses will become heightened both as player
and as audience. Such qualities are clearly defined and illus-
trated in this book. Through searching questions and answers, it
attempts to grasp the essence of the elusive orchestral performer.
By analysing and distinguishing those qualities, you will be able to
discern what it is possible to learn as opposed to what is intrinsic
to the mind of the musician.

A wide spectrum of needs have been addressed, from the rudimentary skills that are necessary in a student right up to the highly
specialized requirements of the young professional.

For parents of budding artists, advice and direction are given to enable their children to go on to prepare themselves for their unique future. To cater for different temperaments among performers, various aspects of education are discussed, ranging from the suitability of your teacher to the question of how to attempt to gain a coveted place at a music college, or whether to opt for the stability of university life instead.

If you are a member of the audience reading this, you may cast your mind back to the days of your own instrumental lessons. With rose-tinted spectacles, you may recall the joys of Bach and Handel, and question your motives for giving it all up. At this point, however, more than likely, a dark shadow will descend and engulf you as you recall that passage which needed just too much work, those rhythms that definitely eluded you, and that dreaded scale-practice. Practising scales is in fact necessary for developing any technique and for understanding musical language, although it is a constant source of battle between most students and their mentors. The book will enlighten you, and inform and enrich your concert experience. It may even inspire you to pick up your instrument again where you left off.

If you are curious about taking up a career in an orchestra, it is imperative for you to understand how the profession works. In this guide, you will learn what to expect and what will be expected from you when you play in an orchestra. As a student at music college, it will be an essential aid that should accompany you to your lessons and rehearsals; and if you are at the stage of auditioning for orchestral jobs, or just starting up in the profession, there are invaluable insights to be found in the following chapters and advice that will help you navigate the inevitable minefields that you will encounter. Aspiring soloists, chamber musicians and teachers will also find the book useful since many of the ensemble and performing techniques discussed can be applied in all musical contexts.

I have used my many years of experience as a principal player in an orchestra, and as a teacher, to illustrate my philosophy and my beliefs in this wonderful and extraordinary profession; and, even though I am a flautist, I have written this work for *all orchestral instruments*. To help me in my quest, I have interviewed many musicians from all the different instrumental sections of the orchestra. These have included rank and file players and principals and freelancers, along with specialist instrumentalists, music scholars and people involved in orchestral management, in order to provide the reader with the widest and most comprehensive view of orchestral life possible.

Except in the chapter entitled *The Formative Years*, I have assumed you have already attained a certain level of proficiency with your particular instrument: that you can produce beauty with a flexible and expressive sound, and execute impeccable rhythm with a good technique and crisp, clear articulation. I have also taken it for granted that you are 'musical'. This is a multi-layered term, but for our purposes think of it as the quintessential, enigmatic quality of musicians communicating through their art. However, merely 'being musical' without those skills will lead to frustration as performers will never seem able to capitalize fully on their God-given talents. Conversely, all the facility in the world without 'musicality' will lead to frustration in the audience, and it will leave the performer feeling confused and empty.

To succeed, you will need all these qualities and more – to be able to go beyond mastery of your instrument, and to learn the disciplines and subtlety you require to become a mature orchestral musician.

The idea for this book came through my teaching at the Royal Northern College of Music, where I am a Senior Lecturer. I have also conducted orchestral rehearsals, and I regularly give lectures on orchestral playing and technique. It was while taking these classes that it became apparent to me that pupils who had reached an advanced standard needed additional information that was not available. They wanted to know about different audition techniques; where to look for jobs; how to continue improving after college; how to discover ways of coping with their nerves; and how to make their sound blend with others. Their questions were abundant, their hunger for knowledge insatiable. I hope my book will help them.

Many musical ideas and thoughts are abstract, subjective and continually shifting. There are no absolutes in music, and this book conveys my own personal viewpoint.

The chapters are in logical order. But you can in fact 'dip in and out' of them without any problem. For easy reference, the most important tips throughout the book have been preceded with:

- (a large dot)

Acknowledgements

Special thanks are due to my colleagues who gave up valuable time to be interviewed in taped conversations between November 2002 and June 2003. Many of the contributors are from my own orchestra, the BBC Philharmonic. It would have been impossible with my performing schedule to go much further afield. The interviews produced marvellous insights into the profession that concurred with many of my own ideas and practices. There were also some minor contradictions which I have intentionally left in.

Biographical details of those interviewed appear below. The interviews are indented throughout the book.

I sincerely thank the following musicians for their candour, and for offering us such important perspectives on the profession and allowing me to illustrate my book with fragments of their lives which I believe are relevant to the reader:

Patrick Addinall has been Principal Trumpet with the BBC Philharmonic for twenty-two years and studied at the Royal Northern College of Music (RNCM), where he is now a Senior Lecturer.

Roger Bigley was the viola player in the Lindsay String Quartet for eighteen-and-a-half years, after which he joined my orchestra as Co-Principal Viola. Presently, he is the Assistant Head of Strings at the RNCM.

John Bradbury has been Principal Clarinet with the BBC Philharmonic for seven years and is a Senior Lecturer at the RNCM. John was previously second clarinet with the Chamber Orchestra of Europe and also with the London Symphony Orchestra. He read Natural Sciences at Cambridge University.

Rachel Brown studied modern flute at the RNCM. She won the international flute competition held by the National Flute Association of America in 1984. She teaches baroque flute and baroque style for modern flautists at the Royal College of Music and the Birmingham Conservatoire, and lectures in classical studies at the Guildhall School of Music and Drama. Rachel is in great demand as a soloist, and as a chamber and orchestral musician, playing on original instruments with the Academy of Ancient Music, the Hanover Band, the King's Consort, London Baroque and the London Handel Players. She has made numerous solo recordings, notably concertos by C.P.E. Bach and Quantz, and recital discs of French Baroque music and Schubert on instruments of the relevant period. She is the author of *The Early Flute* published by Cambridge University Press, and has contributed cadenzas to the new Bärenreiter edition of the *Mozart Flute Concertos*.

Robert Chasey has been our Principal Second Violin for twenty-six years, and he trained at the Royal Manchester College of Music. Previously, he held a position in the Orchestra of the Royal Ballet.

Tim Chatterton graduated from the RNCM in 1986 and works as a freelance trombone player in Manchester. He was an elected member of the Executive Committee of the Musicians' Union from 1991 to 2003.

Fiona Cross is a solo clarinettist who freelances with various chamber groups and orchestras. She is Principal Clarinet with Manchester Camerata and English Sinfonia, and she is a tutor at Trinity College of Music.

Victoria Daniel has been my second flute for eight years, and she studied at the Royal College of Music (RCM).

Peter Dixon is Principal 'Cellist with the BBC Philharmonic, a position he has held for thirteen years. He was formerly a member of the Royal Philharmonic, both as a rank and file player and as their 'number three'. He trained at the Royal Academy of Music (RAM).

Nic Dowton has been a freelance flautist for six years and studied at the RNCM.

Dr David Fanning studied on the Joint Course run between the RNCM and the University of Manchester. Presently he is Professor of Music at the University of Manchester. As a music critic, David has written for the *Guardian* and the *Independent*, and he is currently with the *Daily Telegraph* and the *Gramophone*.

Jonathan Goodall has been our Principal Horn for thirty-one years. He studied at the Royal Manchester College of Music and is now a Senior Lecturer at the RNCM.

Julian Gregory has been a violinist with the BBC Philharmonic for twenty years. He attended Chetham's School of Music and then went on to study at the RNCM.

Ben Hudson is a freelance bassoonist who studied at the RNCM and at the Universität der Künste in Berlin.

Helena Miles is our Orchestral Co-ordinator or 'fixer'.

Brian Pidgeon has been General Manager of both the BBC Philharmonic and the Royal Liverpool Philharmonic. Prior to that Brian was a freelance percussionist.

Emma Ringrose is our second oboist and studied at the RNCM.

Miriam Skinner has been a rank and file 'cellist with us for nine years and studied at the RAM.

Linda Verrier is a Senior Woodwind Lecturer at the RNCM. As a flute-player, she has freelanced with many orchestras and chamber groups as well as touring and recording radio broadcasts as a solo performer. Linda was a prize-winner in an international solo competition held in New Orleans, in the USA.

Tim Williams is a freelance percussionist who studied at the RNCM. He is founder and Artistic Director of and player with Psappha, a contemporary chamber ensemble based in the North-West. He is also director of the International Concert Series at Lancaster University.

In addition, there is an anonymous contributor marked AC in the auditions chapter. At the date of publication, all biographical details were correct.

I would like to acknowledge the use of the following sources: the *Oxford English Dictionary*, the *Encyclopaedia Britannica*, the *New Larousse Encyclopaedia of Mythology* published by Hamlyn, and *Shostakovich: the Man and his Music*, edited by Christopher Norris and published by Lawrence and Wishart, London. Donald J. Grout's *A History of Western Music*, published by J. M. Dent and Sons Ltd, and the *Grove Concise Dictionary of Music*, published by Macmillan, were used for historical accuracy.

The Musician's Guide to Perception and Cognition by David Butler, published by Schirmer Books, and *Phänomene des Musikalischen Hörens (Music, Sound and Sensation)* written by Dr Fritz Winckel, originally published in 1960 by Max Hesses Verlag, were consulted for scientific information.

An article describing the difference between stress and strain is from *Indirect Procedures: A Musician's Guide to the Alexander Technique* written by Pedro De Alcantara, published by Oxford University Press, and an illustration of how the subconscious interprets negative thoughts comes from Don Greene's *Performing Success: Performing Your Best Under Pressure*, published by Routledge. A visualization-learning technique that I have been advocating for many years was confirmed in the BBC television series *The Human Mind*, written and presented by Professor Robert Winston; and supplementary information I required on different temperaments was gathered from the following websites: Howard Stoess's 'History of Tuning and Temperament' and Chris Tyler's 'Musical Tuning and Temperament in Glorious Technicolor'.

Additional anecdotes come from *The Orchestra Speaks* by Bernard Shore, published in 1938 by Longmans, Green and Co., and *Stokowski: A Profile* by Abram Chasins, published by Robert Hale Ltd. A fictional excerpt on counting is taken from *Philharmonic* by Herbert Russcol and Margalit Banai, published by Coward McCann and Geoghagen, Inc, New York, whilst an extract illustrating the right personality for the orchestral profession is from a Canadian pamphlet entitled *Auditions are Just the*

Beginning: A Career Guide to Orchestras by Wendy Reid and Christopher Weait, published by Orchestras Canada (formally the Association of Canadian Orchestras). I am grateful to Roger Turner for re-drawing the musical illustrations, and John Wade for helping me to prepare the harmonic graphs; and appreciation and thanks must also be given to BBC Radio 4 for continually providing me with interesting and relevant facts whilst driving to concert venues.

Quotations that I have not personally found come from *A Dictionary of Musical Quotations* by Ian Crofton and Donald Fraser, published by Croom Helm, and *An Encyclopaedia of Quotations about Music* by Nat Shapiro, published by David and Charles. Appreciation is also given to the following organizations for the use of particular quotes: the Literary Trustees of Walter de la Mare, and the Society of Authors as their representative, the Society of Authors as the Literary Representative of the Estate of Bernard Shaw, the Sir Thomas Beecham Trust Ltd, and Methuen Publishing Ltd.

Every effort has been made to contact the owners of the copyright in the extracts reproduced in this book.

I am indebted to Giles de la Mare, my publisher and editor, for liking the idea in the first place, and also for his support and encouragement as he guided me through this project.

Finally, I would like to thank my family for putting up with me in this incredibly unsociable profession and, above all, the musicians with whom I have played: they have all coloured, shaped and contributed to my musical outlook.

RICHARD DAVIS
Métis-sur-Mer, August 2004

Chapter 1

Introduction to
the Orchestral Profession

'Music is the thing of the world that I love most.'
Samuel Pepys, *Diary*, 1666

Occasionally during a boring rehearsal which seems to be going nowhere, achieving little and stimulating no one, I ask myself: 'Why on earth am I doing this?' Orchestral musicians can easily become disillusioned and question whether they are bringing anything of value into this world.

'The professional musician, as such,
can have no special social status.'
Bernard Shaw, 1856–1950,
Irish dramatist and literary critic

We are not feeding starving people or saving lives. Nevertheless, it has been the arts that have separated the human race from other animals, crossing language barriers with ease, and enriching and inspiring man for millennia. Recent studies have suggested that man may have even sung to communicate before talking, and prehistoric bone flutes and cave paintings are well documented.

The ancient Greeks believed that music was part of everyday life and an essential activity in the pursuit of truth and beauty. Their rich mythology weaves stories of gods, demi-gods and immortals who are masters of the art of music. These deities give a deep insight into the human psyche, reflecting, as they do, the power, magic, love and fascination that music and the arts command, and revealing the human need for visions of the divine cosmos.

As we transport ourselves forward in time to a more scientific age, we may observe the relationship of mathematics and music proposed by Pythagoras. He believed that music and arithmetic were not separate and that both were governed by the laws that determined the whole physical and spiritual universe. The value and power of music were also revered by Aristotle and Plato who acknowledged that art should be kept within strict confines lest it have an immoral influence on human character and society. Even in more modern times, dictators have felt this same need for mandatory control over music, for music *is* power and musicians wield control. It is music that can pierce the heart in an instant and cleanse the soul. Music can calm and it can excite. It can make a strong man weep and a sad man smile. That is power, and we hold that power in our hands. Through our instruments, we create, we interpret and we harness all emotions. Therefore, we musicians shouldn't devalue our worth – we have much to contribute to civilization.

What we produce as musicians, though, is not tangible. It vanishes immediately into the ether, only becoming temporarily etched into the aural memory of the listener. The moment a musician plays a note or turns a phrase is the moment it is 'lost', perhaps in a similar way to a culinary masterpiece which is savoured by the taste buds of a minority of connoisseurs. The majority, if given the chance, would no doubt just gobble up the creation within seconds without a moment's thought or consideration of the long hours it took to prepare. In our case, however, the majority of the audience do appreciate the music we play to them even if we still get the occasional: 'What's your proper job?' and 'What do you do during the day?' My wife was recently at the Royal Albert Hall, attending a Promenade Concert in which I was playing. Beside her sat two elegant ladies, one of whom was educating the other: 'Of course, they don't get paid for performing you know, although I do believe the leader gets a little something!' Maybe she was recalling the argument with the musicians at Juliet's funeral:

> 'Music with her silver sound,
> because musicians have no gold for sounding.'
> William Shakespeare, 1564–1616,
> *Romeo and Juliet*, act IV, scene V

Orchestral musicians spend hours each day practising, rehearsing, performing and travelling; suffering the wrath of conductors; and preparing for the onslaught of critiques in the following day's newspapers. It is easy for us to feel we are an insignificant cog in an unappreciated note factory.

But then, once in a blue moon, we will feel effortlessly in control of our instruments, which will no longer be an appendage we hold onto for dear life but instead will become fused naturally to our bodies. This will not just be a matter of our playing well, for the performance will have attained a higher level as if possessed by a greater force. Dynamics, pitch, colour and expression will be produced as if conjured up by pure desire. There will be no technical problems because there will appear to be a cognitive link between the music, the mind and the body. The notes on the soulless, flat sheet of manuscript paper will spring to life and become animated in the way originally intended. Only when such a summit has been reached will we become 'as one' with our instruments, linked to another dimension, close to the spirit of the composer.

It doesn't matter if no one notices. To have reached this level is reward enough. But this is not the end of the story, for there is an extra dimension to attain and one that is even more desirable. Orchestral musicians are team players, consciously willing *every* member to perform in this heightened state, and longing to be directed by a genius with intellect and brilliance in a concert hall that is an acoustic sensation. This is the ecstatic goal to which we all aspire: when all the orchestral jigsaw pieces fit deliciously into place. As you might imagine, it is not attained often, but when it is, the feeling of euphoria it generates, along with the release and surge of an adrenalin and dopamine cocktail, is like the elixir of life. It gives us that emotional, spiritual and physical recharge that we so desperately yearn for to enable us to continue.

> The good moments are great and make life worth living, but there is a lot of pain you have to go through to win that reward.
>
> Jonathan Goodall

When such a level of musicianship is touched, it becomes clear why we play in this overworked and underpaid profession. All the petty gripes pale into insignificance.

> The monotony of being a rank and file player does get to me sometimes as I crave for more creativity and responsibility; but occasionally we do an amazing concert and I say to myself, 'I'm quite happy to be a rank and file player today because that was a wonderful experience.'
>
> Miriam Skinner

I keep practising because I too crave for this musical ecstasy. We all strive for perfection although we know that reaching such a goal is impossible. In the past, artists have sometimes added minor faults to their creations when they felt they were closing in on perfection, for they knew that only God could attain such flawless excellence. I'm sure musicians wouldn't have worries about such problems. If perfection was possible, we'd make sure we'd achieve it.

What Are the Chances of Success?

It seems to me that there are too many people, playing too many instruments, going for too few jobs. When I was studying, there were fifty other 'cellists at my college alone, and to think that only around two jobs come up a year!

Miriam Skinner

At the Royal Northern College of Music, I give a lecture to the fresher flute students on the statistics of getting a job in a major symphony orchestra. I believe it is better for them to be aware of the cold reality and the harsh facts. Some of them may be put off by their slim chances of getting a job. On the other hand, if they have any hope of surviving in the shark-infested waters of the orchestral profession, they may be spurred on regardless.

You have to ask yourself the following questions. How many players of your particular instrument are required in an orchestra? For example, if you are a horn player, most UK symphony orchestras will have around five members, whereas in the larger German orchestras there could be up to nine contracted players with three of them sharing the principal role. If you are a violinist in Britain, then thirty (sixteen firsts and fourteen seconds) is the standard complement in a large orchestra, and if you are a woodwind player, you would have either three or four players in each section.

How many full-time orchestras are there in your country, and how often do vacancies for your instrument come up? These are worthwhile questions because if you count up the number of orchestras, including opera, ballet, chamber and symphony orchestras, there are quite a few. However, when you look for vacancies, they will not be so abundant. On the Continent, they will appear more frequently, especially in Germany, where many small towns have their own professional symphony orchestra. Logically, you would think that the ratio of populace to orchestra would remain the same relatively, but this is not always the case. Finland, with a population of around five million, boasts twenty-seven full-time orchestras, whereas Scotland with a slightly higher population has only five.

Finally, consideration must be given to the popularity of your instrument if you are to work out how many competitors you will be up against when applying for a vacancy. My orchestra has seen the number of applications for a job range from 120 down to only eight, depending on which section was being advertised.

If you look at the number of music students entering college and observe how many of them actually succeed, what you will see is a pressure-cooker without a release valve. The music colleges are churning out an abundance of string players: if they were all to play symphonic music professionally, six new orchestras would have to be created each year to employ them. The wind, brass and percussion players that they are producing are so plentiful that you could fill an orchestra nine times over. On the South Bank Sinfonia website, they claim that only five per cent of new graduates gain full-time positions in orchestras. So the competition is tough, and it is continually increasing.

Assuming that you are, nonetheless, in the musical marketplace, there is another factor that is often overlooked. It is not just the new graduates who will apply for jobs. While many students at college are capable of playing professionally, and several will be going for jobs towards the end of their course, the wider competitive spectrum includes graduates from the last thirty years, some of whom will have become established freelancers and some already be in orchestral positions. You will be competing against them all and judged by their standards.

Once you have done these highly relevant calculations for your particular instrument, you will soon realize that the statistical probability of your getting a job is heavily against you. And that is before we have discussed ways of improving your playing. Of course, there could be a freelance career open to you. But you would probably find it easier to play in a professional football team.

There were three of us in my year, and I'm the only one playing professionally! Only one was successful from the year above, and no one at all is playing from the year below.

Emma Ringrose

At all times in this profession you will need to hang onto your sense of humour. A friend of mine once made a droll but wise observation. It still makes me smile. It was after a particularly bad class in my first week at music college, and I was upset with the way I had played. We were standing in the dinner queue, and he said: 'Don't worry, it'll probably get worse!' While the second part is not necessarily true, 'don't worry' is the most useful thing anyone has ever said to me.

Chapter 2

The Formative Years

> 'You cannot imagine how it spoils one
> to have been a child prodigy.'
> Franz Liszt, 1811–86

Envisage yourself as a talented young musician at an ordinary school – perhaps the most advanced player on your instrument in the region. You are thinking of embarking on a career in music, but where do you go for guidance?

I regularly come across parents who are faced with this question, and anxious to do the right thing. Desperate for advice that will tell them about all the available options, they are hoping to maximize their child's potential and improve their chance of achieving a career in music and playing the instrument they have heard being practised and enjoyed over the years. They may have spent a fortune buying instruments and even more on tuition fees. Now they want to know whether their child may be able to get into music college. We have seen what the odds are on getting a full-time performing job in an orchestra, but gauging whether a child will get into music college is not easy. Potential becomes a very important part of the equation, and that is difficult to assess in the twenty minute 'snapshot' of an audition. At this age, children develop at varying rates, and you can never predict when their development will stagnate or accelerate. The exceptionally talented musician will appear like a beacon on a clear night and will always get into music college. But I have come across many young players who have been told by their teachers that they are in this elite category when in reality they are far from it. If you are serious about going to music college, it is wise to have your standard assessed by someone who regularly hears talented children.

• *Contact a music college, and apply for an advice audition.*
An 'advice audition' will be taken by a specialist in your field.

It will be in the form of a lesson and provide an honest evaluation of your standard. There will be no guarantees, of course, but it should give you a clearer idea of your potential and your chances for the future. More often than not, requests for advice auditions are made too late in the day, perhaps as close as six months to an entrance audition for music college. That will usually be too late for you to be able to rectify your most serious faults in time. Your assessor may offer constructive general criticism, or perhaps advice on particular exercises that would enable you to improve, but on the big question, only a comment of 'yes', 'no' or varying degrees of 'maybe' can be offered. Ideally students should have such auditions a whole year or more before applying, with the prospect perhaps of a couple of follow-up lessons in between. Continual assessment of a student's progress over a period of time is likely to be the most accurate.

• *Join an organization that specializes in your instrument.*

Such societies and groups exist for all instruments, and your teacher will be able to give you the relevant information. Music shops and websites also carry details of them. You will receive quarterly magazines filled with articles relating to your instrument that offer performing advice, reviews of concerts, new publications, profiles on famous players, details of courses that take place during the school holidays, and much more. There will also be organized events throughout the year, such as weekend courses with master classes, concerts and stalls selling instruments. If you live and are taught in a 'vacuum', it is often difficult to judge your standard; but through attending these events you will make friends, be inspired and hear your competition. Playing any instrument requires perseverance and determination; so don't be disheartened when you hear better players than yourself. Let this encourage and stimulate you to practise even harder.

Persistence

If you are a self-conscious performer, don't give up and indulge in the folly of Athena. In Greek mythology, the goddess Athena, daughter of Zeus, was said to have invented the flute by piercing holes in a stag's horn to replicate the sound made by the dying Medusa (a gorgon), whose throat had been slit by Perseus.

Gorgons were monstrous winged creatures with large projecting teeth, round faces and snakes for hair. When she imitated this creature's fading cries on her new instrument, she was laughed at by the Olympians as she puffed out her cheeks and pursed her lips. Angered by this response, she tossed it aside and cursed anyone who dared pick it up.

- *Inner confidence in your ability is an important quality to have as an aspiring musician, for you need the strength to continue when criticized.*

There is a wise adage: never read what the critics write. But for many performers the temptation is too great. In the *Alternative Careers* chapter, there is an interview with a music critic which attempts to understand his perspective (page 227). If you find yourself reading reviews of concerts, use your own judgment and take what they say with a pinch of salt.

Music Competitions

> 'Pay no attention to critics.
> No statue has ever been put up to a critic.'
> Jean Sibelius, 1865–1957

Competitions and festivals can help you improve your virtuoso skills, but beware of the emotional roller-coaster you may be on. Above all stay focused on your ultimate goal of playing the music whether you win or lose. Although competitions are not conducive to the most natural music-making, they are an inevitable by-product of our profession.

Returning to Athena's cursed flute, let us remember what happened at the very first music competition. Marsyas, a Satyr (half man, half beast) picked up the discarded instrument and learned to play it, enchanting all who heard him. Full of confidence from the praise and attention he was receiving, he dared to challenge Apollo, god of light, prophesy, music and song, to a musical contest. Apollo accepted, opting to play his favoured instrument, the lyre – a plucked stringed instrument that was held to the side of the body, and symbolized wisdom and moderation among the ancient Greeks. Apollo selected King Midas to be the adjudicator, and the competition commenced. Poor old Midas had only narrowly escaped after his last indiscretion when he made the wish that all he touched should be turned to gold. After the musical duel was over, he announced that Marsyas had won. It was a decision he paid for dearly. You may not always agree with the subjective views of a panel, but when entering any competition, you must accept the jury's decision as final. Apollo thought otherwise. He immediately planted a pair of ass's ears on Midas. The fate of Marsyas, the winner, was more gruesome. He was tied to a tree and flayed alive, after which his body was left to fester, suspended from a cave entrance. Some musicians just hate losing.

• *Enjoy the challenge of music competitions, but also face the consequences.*

My teacher believed that you had to be totally obsessed at such an age to stand a chance of getting into music college, and I think he was right. As you make strides in your progress, there will come a time when the next hurdle will have to be addressed.

Is Your Teacher Right for You?

Teachers are of course one of the most important influences in your life. They have the power to stimulate and encourage, and set you off down the road to becoming the best musician you could possibly be. On the other hand, they may destroy and obliterate any prospects you may have of succeeding. There is a thin line between the two because children are vulnerable and easily influenced. Hence, finding the right teacher for a talented and gifted student requires a great deal of thought, and also agreement between parent, child and teacher. Flexibility that caters for the child's needs and idiosyncrasies is paramount in a successful relationship. I should point out that there are some excellent teachers who are infinitely inspirational and are capable of teaching one person for a lifetime without any hint of monotony. But this is a rarity.

• *Are they specialists on your instrument?*

Sometimes we get an applicant for flute who is still being taught by an oboist or a clarinettist. This is fine in the early stages of learning but not acceptable at music-college entrance level.

• *Is my teacher really pushing and getting the most out of me?*

Often, the relationship between pupil and teacher becomes close after a few years, which may be fine if the pupil is excelling and there is still electricity in the lessons. But sometimes stagnation creeps in insidiously, and a move of teacher is for the best. I have known teachers who have not passed on talented pupils, and kept them under their wing, for their own gain and glory, hoping to promote their own teaching skills rather than doing what is best for them. I have also come across the other extreme: for example, a young student who had been playing for seven years, and in that time had had seven teachers. Changing teachers this often can be equally destructive and very confusing to a young mind, since each teacher will probably say different things, some of them cancelling out what previous tutors have said. But, although essential, establishing stability carries the danger that it may lead to monotony.

Quality of Instrument

As you consider a career in music, it is vital for you to acquire a metronome (see 'Rhythm' in the *Ensemble* chapter, page 96), a tuning machine (see *Intonation*) and a decent instrument: a good one will make you play better, while with a wonderful instrument your future will know no bounds. Your standard will determine the quality of instrument you require. One that is below your level will hold you back, and one that is above it will help you to excel. Even at an early stage, musicians often talk about the substantial amounts of money that will be required to buy the next grade of instrument, and so I'm afraid that you may need sympathetic parents who will be willing to re-mortgage. Winning some competitions might cover part of the expense, and perhaps contacting your local authority for financial support might be a good idea too, as scholarships are sometimes available. I have noticed whilst conducting the interviews for this book that it has been the 'proactive' type of person who has generally been successful. They have approached their problems with optimism and thought, tackling obstacles as soon as they appear on the horizon, and, as a result, have found things relatively straightforward. For example, they have gone to libraries and found countless numbers of competitions to enter. They have picked up the names of contacts in books, which have led to them performing in concerts, and they have written to societies and foundations that are willing to give them money. Why don't you do the same?

Assuming the money for a better instrument is there, the next question I often hear parents and children ask is: 'Why don't we buy the best possible instrument now so that it will last for a life-time, and eliminate this time-consuming process every few years?' Finding an instrument that will satisfy a player for their entire musical life is difficult. Improving your instrument slowly but surely is not only a practical solution that will meet your develop-ing needs. It will also cushion the financial pressure.

How Dear Can They Be?

When orchestras tour abroad, the authorities have to know precisely what is entering and what is leaving each country. Instrumental vans have been stopped at check-points between two countries for something as minor as an extra bow in a violinist's case that wasn't registered on the official inspector's list. Some-times customs-officers become extremely authoritarian. Once, as I passed through an airport customs, an armed guard decided he needed to verify what I was cradling in my arms. He beckoned me over and proceeded to grab my flute from my hands. He quickly opened the box, picked up the main body of the instrument and maliciously bent the trill keys. I felt helpless and was in a state of shock as I witnessed my £12,000, 1864, antique Louis Lot flute being manipulated like a coat-hanger.

To illustrate further the costliness of instruments, we were tour-ing South America a few years ago and the local customs men unexpectedly demanded to be told the value of each and every instrument we had before we were granted admission. I happened to be standing beside the solo 'cellist for the tour, and he seemed agitated by this request. Under his breath, he whispered to me: 'If I tell them how much this instrument is worth, I'll never see it again!' I suggested that he put forward a much lower figure while remaining realistic. 'Good idea,' he said. 'I'll tell them it is only worth two hundred thousand pounds, then.' Musicians of this calibre are often loaned the instruments they perform on, and you may see their benefactors' names credited in concert programmes.

Players who have jobs can sometimes get interest-free loans

from their orchestra to obtain that 'career-advancing' instrument. But at this stage I think you will have to rely on generous grandparents to lend you a few thousand pounds. If you choose wisely, a good instrument could be an investment. Therefore, always seek professional advice so that you can find the most appropriate instrument for you. Don't do as I once did when I persuaded my parents to buy the shiniest flute in the shop. I had to get rid of it six months later as it was totally unsuitable for me.

Stolen Instruments

Visit any international concert hall and you will find that their notice-board will probably have a desperate plea for the return of a beloved instrument. Instrumental theft is rife, and you can find websites that help to reunite musician and instrument by advertising all the relevant details.

Frequent orchestral tours, when they travel with valuable instruments, make musicians inevitable targets for thieves. Even on their own turf, every player, if not already a victim, will know several people who have been. Hotel lobbies, the touring coach, dressing rooms and even the concert platform have all been the scene of such crimes, and although your insurance will cover the material cost of replacement when you lose your instrument, an intimate relationship will be unexpectedly severed. Finding a worthy replacement may take years, and so I urge you not only to insure adequately the instrument you love but also to take great care where it is left at all times. Always ask the question: is it as safe as it can be? In a similar vein, during rehearsal breaks (no pun intended) check that your colleagues can manoeuvre through the orchestra without having to climb over or 'shimmy' too close to your instrument. Accidents can occur in the instrumental maze that is created every time a break is announced. The myriad of instruments often resembles an assault course, with instruments being casually placed on the floor or precariously balanced on the edges of chairs. One clumsy step can cost thousands of pounds.

I was writing this during a foreign tour with my orchestra, and by an unfortunate coincidence what I wrote was a timely illustration. Only two hours later, a £10,000 viola was taken from the green-room during our concert interval in Frankfurt.

Wrong Notes

Students frequently play pieces with an infestation of wrong notes, and sometimes they can be totally unaware that their interpretation is erroneous. In such cases, the mistakes will have become deeply embedded in their minds: they will be accustomed to hearing the incorrect notes and they will often end up preferring their own version to that of the composer. Such mistakes will take a long time to rectify. They will have to be unlearned before the correct version can be absorbed. Otherwise inaccuracies will always creep back.

• *When learning a new piece, learn it slowly, making sure the correct notes are played right from the start. This will save time later.*

Learn the Score

Whenever possible, learn a piece (solo or orchestral) from the whole score. Otherwise you will be viewing the work from a narrow perspective. Even if you have the solo part throughout, the picture will be incomplete and distorted. An actor is sent the entire script for a new play so that he can understand the relevance and context of his words in the plot. We too need to know our music in such depth so that our melodic dialogue makes sense. Once learnt, it is not necessary for you to continue studying the piece in this manner all the time as the other part or parts will have become etched into your brain.

Goals

I think that the setting of general goals at all stages of your career is a good idea so long as you also have mini-goals as well. These are smaller and friendlier goals, spaced closer together to make them easier to accomplish.

Recordings are often an important influence in a student's formative years. I spent many a Sunday afternoon listening to my treasured record collection of 'flute gods' and orchestral lollipops, studying different styles and interpretations, and immersing myself in the music and the scores. I distinctly remember listening to a record of one of my idols when I was only fourteen. Knowing that I would never play at that standard, I simply wished that I could play the notes in the piece. Such modest, bite-sized goals are fairly easily reached, and stimulate the desire to make progress.

• *Each target you set and attain will motivate you for the next challenge.*

The law of diminishing returns dictates that, as you excel, it becomes more difficult to make noticeable progress. A beginner will progress by leaps and bounds, whereas a professional may take months to improve by a meagre but desirable one per cent. At this stage, though, your mini-goals may be passing the next exam, playing in a local concert or festival, learning to articulate more clearly, or memorizing three scales. Whatever you decide to focus on, and follow through, will help you gain ground, and bring your ultimate goal closer.

As you improve on your instrument, be aware that it is easy to become excessively focused and insular, and to assume that playing with other instrumentalists would waste your time. You may be able to play well, but if you can't play with other people, you will have forgotten why you took up music in the first place. So right from the beginning it is important to:

Play Music With and For People

At an early stage, try and persuade your teacher to play duets with you. When the duet book was taken down from the shelf during my lessons, it was like receiving candy for all the hard work I had done. Playing with a good musician immediately makes you play better: your ears begin to open when you listen to the sound they make, their articulation and their musicality. You will hear harmonies and experience intonation, and begin to acquire the basics of ensemble technique. Playing duets can also benefit the teacher: it can highlight the strengths and weaknesses of the pupil. I occasionally play them with my college students. It allows me to focus and assess subtleties that may not be apparent when they play solo. It can give me a clear indication of their suitability and their possible development towards a professional level.

This book is primarily about becoming an orchestral musician, and so you really should play in an orchestra as soon as you can to see whether you like it.

• *Join your local youth orchestra.*

Look in the *Rhinegold Guide to Music Education* and find out where it rehearses and auditions. After hearing the sound of my own county youth orchestra, and experiencing the excitement of public performances together with the touring and socializing, I was convinced that this was what I wanted to do for the rest of my life.

If you improve immeasurably, there is the National Youth Orchestra and the European Union Youth Orchestra to consider, both of which play at a very high level. They hold extremely competitive annual auditions, and are the cream of the youth-orchestra world.

Ensemble playing is imperative for any musician's success: you have the opportunity to play wonderful music; you hear the blending of instrumental colours; and you go beyond the exercises studied in lessons with your teacher. What I say should not be misinterpreted. Such exercises should remain vitally important to you for technical improvement, for gaining control and consistency, and for initiating a lifetime programme of practice.

Music School

You may wish to audition for a Saturday music school where like-minded children group together at a major music college. Here they can have individual lessons on their principal instrument and piano tuition, in addition to theory and ensemble sessions. Lessons at these schools may be at the future college of your choice, but, more than likely, the tutors won't be the top professors from the senior faculty, and will play no part in assessing your application for a place at that institution once you leave school. All the same, the top Saturday music schools boast an enviable success rate, by anyone's standards, for getting their students into music college.

There are many secondary schools in the country with excellent music departments, and around 250 independent schools that offer music scholarships. But you may decide to go one stage further and apply to one of the top specialist music schools. Some children flourish at these schools as they can be stimulated by learning alongside the most musically gifted young musicians in the UK. You have to be careful, though, because such intense music-making can sometimes lead to 'burn out' at a very young age as well as discouraging other children from continuing in music. Teachers and parents should look at each child's temperament and personality. Ask whether they would enjoy and profit from the competition. Would they thrive when being pushed, or do they need a broader curriculum along with a less pressured lifestyle at this stage?

The standard of music at the following specialist schools is remarkable, and children will get practice-time scheduled into their timetable along with expert tuition, master classes, and ensemble, orchestral and concert experience. All of them are fee-paying, but through means-testing there are various grants and scholarships of up to 100% to be had. These five schools advertise that they are open to all, irrespective of financial or social background, and that their pupils are admitted solely on the basis of a musical audition. Once again, obtaining a place at one of these institutions does not guarantee admission to music college. Conversely, failing to get into one of them is not necessarily a reflection on your talent and in no way suggests that, as you mature, you won't be likely to succeed in the music profession.

The *Purcell School* is supported by the British Government's Music and Ballet Schools Aided Pupil Scheme and is situated on the fringe of Greater London on a twenty-acre campus. It has 170 pupils aged from seven to eighteen. It has a broad-based curriculum covering the arts and sciences, and it has achieved consistently excellent academic and examination results. *www.purcell-school.org*

St Mary's Music School is surrounded by gardens in the heart of Edinburgh. It opened its doors in 1880 to educate the boys of the Choir of St Mary's Episcopal Cathedral. In 1972 the school widened its intake, allowing in girls and pupils of all faiths, and began to educate not only choristers but instrumentalists and composers as well. The classes are small, the timetable is flexible and tailored to individual needs, and pupils have a wide choice of

subjects. Results, musically and academically, are consistently excellent.
www.st-marys-music-school.co.uk

Wells Cathedral School is unique as it operates within the structure of a conventional, high-achieving, co-educational, day/boarding school with over 750 pupils of which 200 specialize in music.
www.wells-cathedral-school.com

Yehudi Menuhin founded his school for stringed instruments and piano in 1963. The school, situated in Surrey, educates more than 60 children of between eight and eighteen, and in 1973 it was accorded special status as a Centre of Excellence for the Performing Arts. The 'cellist Mstislav Rostropovitch became president of the school after Lord Menuhin's death.
www.yehudimenuhinschool.co.uk

Chetham's School of Music in Manchester was originally founded as a Bluecoat orphanage for 'forty poor boys' in 1653, and started a new life as a specialist, co-educational school for young musicians in 1969. Now, with over 280 pupils, it is still housed in and around the historic fifteenth-century college building, and is at the forefront of music education in Britain and Europe, with students constantly achieving competition success, especially in the BBC's Young Musician of the Year. Although Chetham's is an independent, charitable foundation, more than 80% of its entrants come from Local Authority maintained schools.
www.chethams.com

Julian Gregory began playing the fiddle when he was seven years old and went to Chetham's at the age of eleven. He lived locally and so he didn't board. The year was 1970, when Chetham's was in its early days as a specialist music school.

> For me, Chets was fantastic: I was really lucky that I got my secondary education there, and right from the first year I was put into a quartet with three other good players. The things that bothered me about going to a specialist music school were that my non-musician friends had better gym facilities at their school and that they were building

go-carts and coming home with tables they had made in woodwork. But when I think back to my time at Chets, there is one moment that sticks out and defines the fact that I was very happy there. It was a Wednesday morning, and I was playing in the upper refectory in a small chamber orchestra. The piece was *Jesu, Joy of Man's Desiring* and I had never heard it before in my life. I remember listening to this fantastic music, being part of it and thinking of my other friends at regular school doing maths, English and French, and realizing how lucky I was, and I still have that feeling when I come to work in the orchestra today! I think of all those other people and what they do for a living, and then I think, 'Here am I', and I get the same buzz that I experienced at Chets all those years ago.

It is a privilege to be playing music as a professional and not just as a hobby. I have played in my orchestra for twenty years, and when I walk onto the platform of Manchester's Bridgewater Hall, I feel special. Even though I am part of a section, I know that if I play well, it will be great; and if I play badly, it will have an effect on the performance. The combination of the pressure and tension makes me feel fortunate to be doing this for a living.

Julian Gregory

More information on these specialist music schools and others too can be found in the *Rhinegold Guide to Music Education*.

You Are Not Doing Enough Practice!

It never ceases to amaze me how little daily practice is achieved by school children who aspire to go to music college. When questioned, they will often say it is about an hour. I then ask them: how much practice would they expect a young dancer to be doing at the Royal Ballet School, or how much preparation would a young swimmer who wanted to compete at the next Olympics be accomplishing daily? As the pupils identify with other people in similar circumstances, the reality dawns and everything is put into perspective. The others, with equal pressures, would be highly disciplined, organized and motivated, and would get up early to practise their skills. They would willingly sacrifice such pleasures as television to better their chances. If you as a musician are determined, you will always find time; and if you have the right temperament, you will always enjoy and want to practise. Commitment at this level can only come from within. A regime should never be arbitrarily imposed by either parent or teacher.

Warming Up

As you become more serious about your instrument, and start to practise harder, you will also need to respect your body. Warm-up routines are essential for achieving a long playing life. Depending on your type of instrument, and indeed your 'school' of playing, your teacher will instruct you on what type of warm-up you should develop. For many it will be a combination of long notes, slow scales and melodic leaps. By playing long notes in an intelligent way, you can achieve a host of beneficial results. You can make sure that the instrument is working properly while checking the co-ordination of your fingers. It is surprising how quickly the muscles that are used to playing your instrument seem to forget what they should do as soon as you stop. Playing long, beautiful notes with a variety of dynamics, with extreme diminuendos and crescendos through all registers, will reinforce the brain and strengthen the muscles, and it will lead to consistency and control. While warming up, you might try changing the sounds you make in order to get used to the room you are playing in, and to find a resonance that responds to your instrument. You will notice that the art of sounding good in all acoustics is discussed in several other chapters, and the advice given will prove beneficial when you start to perform. Experimenting with 'tone' in this way will help you reproduce yesterday's sound and then hopefully improve on it. As you advance, you will also discover a new rainbow of colours and together with it a more refined method of production.

Warming up shouldn't be abandoned when you become a professional, nor should practising (see the 'Keeping in Shape' section in the *Surviving in the Orchestral Profession* chapter, page 214). Players who give up a daily routine of this sort will soon begin to feel a deterioration in their playing. A top athlete wouldn't dream of running a race without warming up beforehand. No doubt he would still be able to run fast, but he might get cramp from pushing his muscles hard without stretching first. He would not perform at his best, and he might also suffer the next day. You are no different. But even with a good warm-up routine, musicians are still prone to injuries.

Injuries

I have decided to write about injuries in this chapter because, although most musicians who experience pain do so at music college or later on in the profession, it is often in the early years that the rot sets in. Playing a musical instrument to a high standard requires countless hours of dedicated practice, which the human skeleton is not designed for. Prolonged periods maintaining the same position, as well as enduring intense physical and mental pressure, can result in injuries. Physical pain caused by playing musical instruments is widespread within the orchestral world. Bad posture, overwork, stress and laziness are some of the causes.

• *Check your playing posture.*

Your teacher should address the problem and ensure that your playing posture is one that will last a lifetime. However, lessons are not always where the real problems lie: the danger area is orchestral rehearsals. In a boring rehearsal, you tend to slouch. Too many players sharing a stand may have to strain to read the music. Uncomfortable chairs, long rehearsals and bad lighting can encourage bad habits. So beware!

It is an interesting fact that sitting down puts more pressure on your backbone than standing up. Approximately 100kg of pressure is put upon your spine when you stand properly, but that escalates to around 185kg when you sit down. If you slouch as well, it rockets even higher.

Yoga and Alexander technique are commonly used to correct posture and aid relaxation, while physiotherapy and osteopathy are extensively used when players experience pain. Osteopathy can be controversial, though, as it is still classified as a complementary medicine. There are over 3000 qualified osteopaths in the UK, and it is recognized by conventional medicine as being 'at least as good as anything they have to offer'.

• *Don't practise erratically.*

Erratic practice can lead to injuries and prolong them; yet time and time again, I come across students who habitually skip one day of practice and consider it acceptable to catch up with hours of work the next. This 'stop-start' strategy is barmy. It takes time to build up the physical stamina that is required for you to practise for any length of time. This must be achieved gradually and then be sensibly maintained.

My views about cumulative practice having an exponential effect on one's standard are set out in the 'Practice' section of the *Nerves* chapter on page 114. There I also discuss the benefits of spreading your work out over the day. Inconsistent practice is not always the student's fault, though, but often the outcome of college timetables. If you are only left with small windows of opportunity for practice between lectures, the result will be practice that is crammed and panicky.

> At music colleges today, I worry that the students don't have as much time to practise as we did. They seem to have additional exam pressures and more lectures to attend, and so inevitably something has to go. Perhaps the depth of enjoyment in their learning is sacrificed, and more often than not they succumb to aches and pains, leading to tendonitis, which, from my experience, is definitely on the increase. Some students complain that they have to practise too intensively in between lectures, and cram their work into a ridiculously condensed time-frame, causing tremendous stress on the body. Conversely, as a result of the over-structuring during term-time, when the pace slackens at the end of the year, many students then seem to find themselves at a loss, and incapable of structuring their own timetable.
>
> Linda Verrier

One obsession today is with the need to quantify everything in league tables. Music, however, is unquantifiable unless you bring it down to its most basic level and ask such questions as: is the note right, or is the note wrong? is it sharp, or is it flat? But this only encourages learning the surface elements of the art. Achieving a truly musical performance demands so much more.

> There is no time for experimentation because the students, through conditioning, are more concerned about percentage results in their performances. In my day, results were never published: it was either pass or fail. That relieved a lot of pressure, leaving us time to concentrate on the overall learning process. We could sit in the library, listening to recordings of past players, and digest their styles. [See the 'Study or Mimic' section in the *Performing Philosophies* chapter, page 50.] In music, you have to practise different techniques to play your instrument and then discard them if they don't work for you. There is no 'one way' of doing things in music, and so you have to take 'a line', and follow it for perhaps six weeks or even six months; and even then

it may not work for you; but still, you have to experience it for your-self. It can be frightening to try these sorts of things out when you may appear to an onlooker to be going backwards in standard. As you experiment, finding a true depth of the music while realizing your potential and understanding the possibilities of what can be achieved, takes time.

The best students aren't affected by any of these concerns because they have a creative soul, fuelled by their own internal agenda, that will develop voraciously, no matter.

Linda Verrier

Often, when you say you are in pain, people will brush it aside, thinking it is nothing. But aches and pains in fingers or tingling sensations in arms can be misunderstood. I have encountered doctors who laugh and say: 'Oh, just play through it!' This is bad advice and well past its sell-by date. Look at footballers who come off the field as soon as they have a slight 'twinge'. Modern-day practitioners take into account the duration of a player's career as well as the need to repair their body as quickly as possible.

You should be cautious: some injuries are repairable whilst you continue to play, but others only respond to a total cessation of work – this has been confirmed by physiotherapists while I have been researching this book. I have come across several students who have insisted on playing though such aches, pains and strains, and have ended up having to take a year off from study-ing because playing aggravated their problem.

- *Seek medical advice for all injuries, and if you feel that you aren't being taken seriously, get a second opinion.*

If, through injury, you have taken off a substantial period of time, build your stamina up slowly, as with any recuperation. Anxious musicians, fearful of slacking, may attempt to catch up too quickly and cause themselves further injury.

Music College ...

This is the normal gateway into the profession. It will give you the best tuition and allow you to be totally focused. Most musicians intent on a performing career will apply to one of the main music colleges. So which one should you choose? Your teacher will advise you about the best one for your particular instrument. You may decide to go to a specific college because of the reputation of a particular teacher; but do be aware that teachers sometimes move from one establishment to another. This happened recently with a student who turned up only to find that their intended teacher had moved on.

Go and have a lesson with the teacher of your choice, and see if things are going to work. Hear them play, and, if possible, attend their master classes to see whether you like their style. You must realize, however, that some excellent teachers aren't the best players, and conversely that you can encounter magnificent players who are so instinctive, possessing little idea of how their standard is achieved, that they are not the best people with whom to study. It is also worth noting that not all musicians teach as they play: the renowned flautist Jean-Pierre Rampal was telling a young player about some technical point during a public class when the student retorted: 'But that's not what *you* did in the concert last night!' Rampal replied calmly and sympathetically: 'Do as I preach and not as I play.' I am always telling my students that I teach as I would *dream* of playing.

Even if you don't know what the playing of each professor is like, make sure that you know their names at the audition as well as those of other great players of your instrument. Look as if you are at least showing an interest in studying with them. Do your homework, and if you get offered a place, ask for the teacher of your choice in writing.

... Or University?

If you don't get into a good music college, you may choose to go to university instead. The competition is immense at the top conservatoires, and so going to a university with a good music department may be a better decision for some students.

During music college entrance auditions many hopeful candidates reveal this misconception to us: 'I want to come to music college because there will be more playing opportunities.' Applicants are often under the illusion that being at music college will enable them to participate in orchestral rehearsals day after day. This just isn't the case, especially for wind and brass players. There will be many students of your standard in addition to those in the years above, all of them fighting for those few places in the orchestra; whereas at university you are more likely to be a bigger fish in a smaller pond and therefore be rewarded with more playing.

> What disturbs me about music college is the lack of orchestral training and preparation. The whole ethos of these places seems to guide you in the direction of being a soloist, and if that doesn't work, chamber music will do for you. That is just bonkers. I think that the students are not made aware of the harsh realities of musical life and, conversely, they're not exposed to the real thing enough to appreciate what good fun it can be – I get so much pleasure from orchestral playing that I've never understood people who don't. I was fortunate in that all I ever wanted to be was an orchestral musician. My mother was a freelance 'cellist, and I did take up the 'cello because of her, but she didn't belabour me and lock me up to practise – she was actually very relaxed about it and my desire came from within. Fortunately, too, my teacher was a great orchestral player: in fact that's why I went to him rather than messing around only learning concertos and sonatas to the exclusion of orchestral study that seems to happen now. Most of what I did really was study orchestral technique. I wanted him to teach me what he was best at and not what the Academy perhaps thought he should be teaching me. I do lots of concertos and recitals now, though, but that is not what I set out to do: it has come about as a result of the job that I've got.
>
> Peter Dixon

If you fail to get into music college, or you aren't sure about embarking on a musical career, then a common option is to go to university first. You can apply to do a postgraduate year at a music college after getting your degree; but if this is your plan, make sure that you keep your playing standard high throughout your undergraduate course. University will give you a more rounded education. But for three years you will miss out on the intensive tuition that music college students will be receiving. Even with the best intentions, it is easy to fall behind.

Although it is unusual, our principal clarinet player John Bradbury proved that it is possible to go to university, not study music at all there, and yet still become a professional musician:

> I studied Natural Sciences at Cambridge as I wasn't sure about a career in music at that point in my life. I knew that I could keep my clarinet going while I was at university, because they gave me a bursary

towards private clarinet lessons, which I had in London; and even though I was reading sciences I did *loads* of playing.

Between my second and third year, I got a travel bursary, which I used to study in Chicago for the summer. It was then that I decided that I did want music as my career, and so I applied to do a postgraduate course at the Royal Academy. I thought that the people at music college would have a narrower approach to life; but in some aspects, they were more broad-minded and interesting than the university students. However, you never get something for nothing, and I had missed out on three years of really strong, focused study of the clarinet and therefore fallen behind. In fact, I was lucky to get into music college.

I don't think that you should ever say: 'I wish I had gone to music college,' or 'Should I have gone to university?' Wherever you have gone, if you've made the most of it, then that is good. But I do think that wind players should think very seriously about going to university because of the playing opportunities you will get there. I now teach at a music college, and my students don't usually get to play in an orchestral concert until their third year. We have a large clarinet department and only three places for each concert. At university, the orchestras won't be at the same standard, but they will still be good, and there is far less competition.

John Bradbury

• *You are at college for such a short time.*

As I have mentioned, wherever you go to study, you should make sure your teacher is right for you, someone who will push you and help you at the same time. If your relationship goes sour or you. don't feel inspired, then move on. Don't stay with your tutor for fear of upsetting him. Many people do. Remember, it is your time, your money, your life, and no one else's.

• *Always be 'pro-active'.*

Students at college basically fall into two categories. Type A are players who wait for performing work to fall into their lap. They listen to their contemporaries practising and improving. They blink and find the whole world has moved on. Type B are the 'get up and go' players who study hard, are good at promoting themselves, and make everything work in their favour.

Right from the beginning of college I was pro-active. In my first year, I managed to get together with a pianist and formed a duo. I went to the library and found lists of competitions along with various music societies, which I wrote to, and I got offered concerts straight away. I also entered a competition held by the London Philharmonic, and won. The agent I am with today was in the audience, and we teamed up there and then.

Fiona Cross

Are You Sure You Want to Do This?

Ask yourself this question. Do you really want to perform music as a career? If you have any doubts at this stage, think again, because you should *crave* to be a musician. It must be more important to you than anything in the world, and it should be inconceivable for you to want to consider any other profession.

> Wanting to be a musician is like going into the Church: it is a calling, and if you love music that much, nothing will stop you. We sometimes tell students not to take the plunge as there are few career prospects and there is little money in it; but if they still want to have a go, we must give them the best possible chance.
>
> Roger Bigley

I remember that a few days after I had been offered my job with the BBC Philharmonic, a principal flute player from another orchestra came up to me at a friend's wedding reception. I thought he was going to congratulate me, but instead he said rather gruffly: 'It doesn't get any easier, you know!' Even though he was blunt, he was right, since the work never ends, and while some things do get easier, problems are always cropping up.

> Playing classical music is a double-edged sword as you can never reach perfection. There is no limit to how things can be varied and improved, and that is what makes it a great art. The trouble is that you never quite get there. But that of course makes it interesting as there is always a new challenge.
>
> Patrick Addinall

The Right Personality

This is another problem that is not often thought about in the early years of studying. The type of personality that is best suited to life in an orchestra is highlighted in this extract from a Canadian pamphlet called *Auditions are Just the Beginning: A Career Guide to Orchestras* by Wendy Reid and Christopher Weait:

39

Much more than a strong musical talent is needed to enjoy a successful career in an orchestra. Ambition to succeed must be evident at an early age, and this wish to be involved in music will be an incentive to face many years of hard training.

Discipline is another important attribute. It makes a student practise regularly, with thoroughness and attention to detail, and thus provides the essential groundwork.

Intelligence, coupled with objective self-criticism, is also crucial. In order to develop and learn, a good musician must not overestimate his ability, but always be ready to improve after each performing experience. At the same time, a musician should enjoy a sense of confidence and pride in performing achievements and not be prone to negative attitudes.

Finally, flexibility is important because, as an orchestral musician, you are part of a team and must be able to adjust to changing circumstances. A symphony orchestra is a truly amazing body of people – the largest ever working together as a single unit! Flexibility also helps combat the boredom and stress which may arise. As in many jobs with a certain amount of repetition, boredom and, with that, carelessness can creep in; so be on guard and keep up the discipline. Working in an orchestra is a close and intense relationship, and it is necessary to be co-operative and unselfish. One must be able to both follow and lead.

Reproduced with kind permission of Orchestras Canada (formally the Association of Canadian Orchestras)

Music colleges rarely address such personality issues in terms of whether a player is suitable for the orchestral profession. I believe that, at any given moment, all students should know the entire score. You will always have the right to disagree, and nothing makes me happier than finding out that players whom I had reservations about, are now doing well. However, music colleges usually err on the side of caution and optimism in their assessments, and take past playing into consideration. But in the music profession the *present* is the only thing that matters. How you played at your entrance audition all those years ago is irrelevant; the potential you used to show is immaterial; and the mark you achieved in last month's technical exam is of no consequence. What does matter is how you play under pressure.

- *It is how you play today, and how you play tomorrow, that will build or undermine your reputation.*

We all know that students improve at different rates, and the following scenario is familiar at music college: a star pupil wins all the concertos and gold medals, but for one reason or another reaches a plateau in his playing, which brings his career to a full stop. This story should encourage the less visible students who continue to improve day after day – further than anyone had ever expected – and in time slip effortlessly into the profession.

After College

While you are at college, you are still eligible to play in such groups as the European Union Youth Orchestra, the National Musicians' Symphony Orchestra, the Britten-Pears Orchestra and the Gustav Mahler Jugend Orchester. All of them perform at an astonishing level.

Often students will start applying for jobs in their last year at college. As we have seen, there are very few of these around. But a handful of new, innovative orchestras have evolved in this country and abroad, many of which are aimed at the inexperienced player straight from college. They could be ideal for acquiring the qualities and skills that are described in this book, and help you to become a fully-fledged orchestral musician. Great expense is involved in running full-time orchestras, as I mention in the *Mechanics of the Orchestra* chapter, and you may find that these 'training' orchestras will often not pay well – sometimes just your expenses. But they do offer experience for the inexperienced, and will therefore be more valuable to you than money at this stage, especially if the alternative is living in oblivion, and waiting for the LSO to ring. These orchestras come and go, and the majority are run on a concert-by-concert basis, like the Cardiff Bay Chamber Orchestra; but there are some that offer regular work such as the South Bank Sinfonia in London, which offers a seven-month contract, with many concerts and much education work. There is an orchestral academy in Berlin that is affiliated to the Philharmonic which boasts a 55% success rate in the profession, 25% of the players entering the Berlin Philharmonic itself.

Some musicians decide to apply for 'minor' full-time orchestras on the Continent in order to earn and learn, and while the standards in these may not be the best, they will be serving the local community with concerts and learning the repertoire at the same time.

I have known many musicians who have had full-time jobs in foreign orchestras. If the standard is inadequate, most people will want to return home after a few years. And yet, ironically, the effort required for disengagement may often be greater than that for winning the job in the first place. So there are a number of points to watch out for if you find yourself in this situation. Check your contract. Make sure that you are allowed the freedom to audition for other jobs, and, if successful, that you will be authorized to leave without completing the whole season. If the standard is not high, then, although you may be gaining experience, there will be the danger that your own playing will decline. You tend to play at the level of those around you. Playing with musicians who are considerably better will have a positive effect; but if they are of a much lower standard, life will become difficult. We are adaptable creatures and our senses can become acclimatized to a ragged ensemble and poor intonation. To counteract this, practise and at the same time listen to top recordings in order to keep your ears attuned to the levels to which you aspire. However, if you are a great player, your standard may possibly filter through and help make the orchestra you are playing with one of note.

Before we tackle the technical aspects of getting into an orchestra, you will need to have learnt how to stand out from the crowd: not in an eccentric or overpowering way, but a way that makes the listener yearn for more – and catch their breath through your imagination and skills in communication.

> You've got to remember that every single person performing at this level plays well. They present every orchestral excerpt perfectly and *all* could go in and do the job. Make sure that you can do it better, for playing the notes is not enough. Adding that special something, listening a little bit more, and being extra-sensitive will make *you* stand out.
> Nic Dowton

You will need to be able to play in a way that both captivates the audience and compels them to hear more of your playing. The next chapter explores a few methods that may help.

Chapter 3

Performing Philosophies

Throughout your performing career, you will have to walk onto that stage and play with commitment and passion. You will have to unite with all the members of the orchestra whatever is happening in your personal life. Even if you are in the middle of an argument or feeling unwell, you will have to switch off the troubles in your life, and you will have to learn how to harness your personal emotions and transform the energy behind them so that you can always play at your best.

A Musical Vision

When you are performing music at a professional level, you should already have attained the abilities and skills that are described in the chapters that follow. But there is a final *je ne sais quoi* that is essential for you to succeed and yet is so often missing in students who are aiming for a career in music. I remember my flute teacher telling me that no one under the age of thirty-five could possibly interpret Bach and Mozart in any depth. The belief was that, when young, you are only capable of mimicry and not of true understanding. (See 'CD Culture', later in this chapter, on page 49.) At the time, I found this extreme and irritating, but as I get older, I understand and appreciate his reasoning better. There is a paradox, however: as we do get older and our understanding of music increases, our facility often deteriorates. And so if this hypothesis is true, there may only be a short cross-over period when we can play at the very top level.

The Je Ne Sais Quoi

One method I advocate is playing as if today is the last day of your life and this performance is the one by which audiences will remember you. Many musicians take this approach. But I have recently started looking at my methods from another perspective as well. When a great actor reads a script, he has to perform it in such a way that the audience believes he is doing it for the first time. He has to give the impression that he is speaking naturally, that he is improvising, even though the author has spent an eternity getting the script exactly right. When an actor does this successfully, with impeccable timing, sincerity and finesse, he becomes the character in the plot instead of a mere actor reading lines. I encourage my students to consider this technique, too. When adopting it, they must know precisely what the composer has written, right down to the last detail. But, even so, I ask them to explore the harmonic and thematic changes in the piece and enjoy the resolutions as if hearing them for the first time. I want them to feel surprise at the different directions in which the music travels, free their minds, and play the phrases as if they have no idea what is about to happen. Try playing a piece that you know well, creating such excitement, and giving the impression that the music is alive and has a will of its own. You may find that this approach will add a new spark to your interpretation, and unexpected depth also.

The Journey

Another successful approach I encourage is to do the exact opposite. By this, I mean you should educate the listener: you should pinpoint key changes, and perhaps subtly emphasize where the music is going. Whatever method or combination of methods you use, always take the audience on a journey. You will encounter many intersections on your musical expedition, and your decisions about where you want to go, and what you choose to show us, will become your interpretation. You may have been to that musical destination many times before, but you must still love visiting it and get excited showing others around. You may be guiding us through life-threateningly dangerous terrain in scary passages with an uneasy atmosphere. Perhaps you will then approach a tranquil and comfortable environment with a soothing melody and hushed chords. As a performer, you are the guide and you must keep us with you at all times. Draw us in through your musicality. Don't allow us to drift off elsewhere!

> 'All music seems alike to Toscanini ... everything he plays, he plays as though it were his favourite and adored piece. Lavishing his heart and soul on second-rate compositions, he can make them seem great works of art.'
>
> From *The Orchestra Speaks* by Bernard Shore

Singers in the Coffee Queue

Whatever method you may have adopted for conveying your musical vision, you should also consider how much of your interpretation is actually reaching the listener. Often a lot of it is lost in the concert hall. Rectifying this doesn't mean playing louder all the time. Dynamics make more immediate impact than musicality and so you need to discriminate between volume and musical projection. You must learn this art; otherwise you will continually be forcing rather than inspiring. Actors use their whole bodies as a sounding board so that they can be heard at the back of the theatre whether they speak softly or bellow. If they really whispered, nothing would carry at all; and so they have had to develop different techniques for appearing to have hushed conversations while remaining audible at a distance. It is the same for singers. They learn to use their whole instrument (that is, their bodies) to project their voice. Anyone visiting a music-college refectory will be able to identify a singer at once from the way they ask for a cup of coffee. Breathing deeply, opening up their chest, and with their vocal chords in exactly the correct place for the required intonation, they identify a resonance that will vibrate and be carried a hundred feet away from them, even if they are talking quietly. As an orchestral musician, you will only have to use this skill when playing a solo, but you should acquire it in order to impress an audition panel as well. Many students fall into this trap: they think that one hundred per cent of their sound, their musicality and their personality is conveyed to every corner of the concert hall. And yet most of it will have vanished by the fourth row.

• *Get a friend to listen to you from a distance to see what carries and what is lost.*

Learn to Conduct

Before you present your musical vision to an audience, you must be confident that your interpretation is acceptable, that your rhythm is not distorted, and that there is a natural flow to the work. There should usually be a structural relationship – sometimes a common pulse – between each section of the work, that unites all the movements. All tempi should be interdependent and linked, unless you wish to add the element of 'surprise' to your performance. This principle is particularly relevant if you have trouble deciding on a tempo for a sonata.

> 'I have always been disappointed in the approach to a sonata by players who fix the tempo of each movement without reference to the piece as a whole, as if the piece was composed as a set of unrelated movements. I firmly believe we should attempt a rough unity of pulse, not necessarily exact, but in a similar way that a meal contains complementary dishes. There should be a thread of pulse running through the sonata which binds the musical ideas into a whole.'
>
> Trevor Wye, b.1935,
> flautist, celebrated teacher and author of flute-practice books

Exercises to improve your rhythm are to be found in the *Ensemble* chapter. But in order to maintain a natural flow in general, you should learn to conduct. This will help you rhythmically as well as producing an interpretation that can be accompanied. One of the biggest problems for young players is fitting in with the piano accompaniment. They often feel as if they are playing in a straitjacket. By learning to conduct, your inner pulse is set in motion. You can then get a feel for the infinite musical possibilities and attain a freedom that will allow the music to breathe, and also add breadth to your interpretation. If you can conduct a phrase, a tempo change or a rubato with relative ease, an accompanist will be able to fit in with you as simply as completing a child's jigsaw.

The Composer's Condensed Universe

When performing, never forget about the importance of the composer's own thoughts. Was he inspired by something visual or by emotions: by love, by some belief, or maybe through an epiphany that compelled him to translate his thoughts and feelings into music. Unfortunately musical notation by itself is lifeless. His whole universe, his overpowering emotions are squashed flat. Phrases are trapped in this two-dimensional form, and it is the responsibility of the performer to release them. He must search and discover, and bring the notes to life. Finding out as much about the music and the composer as you can will help; and even if the universe you stumble on in your musical exploration is different from the composer's, it doesn't really matter, since at least the notes will be able to breathe again.

A professor from the Royal Academy told this story about inanimate playing. He had recently attended a 'soul-destroying' audition. Being a dedicated teacher, he had tried to stimulate the mind of the candidate and to coax her into becoming more musical. The sound of a fog horn, he said, was not envisaged by the composer. He described the bittersweet emotions of a man returning to an old family home, a place that had brought great joy to him in his childhood. On reaching it, he had found it to be in a state of dilapidation and a mere shadow of its former glory. The burning red sun set over the woods behind the house as he gazed transfixed at the wreck.

'I understand!' she replied, taking her instrument to her lips and enthusiastically playing like a road-rage man driving a juggernaut down the M1. Without some knowledge of history, without animation, imagination or poetry, music will be two-dimensional – or else plain ugly, as in this case.

Style

Playing in a historical style that is suitable for the composer is vital if you wish to achieve maturity, depth and understanding in your performance. Students regularly perform pieces without any thought or knowledge of their context. They do not have to play on period instruments. But having some knowledge of how they worked and of the various techniques used in playing them, and of the sound they made, will bring new insights into your interpretation. The art of articulation has evolved for centuries, with countless permutations; and yet we use limited markings today. It is your duty to realize those markings in an appropriate manner.

Two common stumbling blocks are staccato and the accent. Staccatos would have been short and dry in one era, and 'bouncy' in another. Accents are personal to each composer. An accent in a work by Stravinsky might need to be played with a harsh, painful stab, whereas Schubert often required them to be played with a 'smile'; and in Mozart's music the accent is often linked to the emotion, excitement and subtlety of a 'thrill'. All markings are relative and they must be investigated.

Ornaments and grace notes are too often executed as if they were a technical exercise, their original purpose forgotten. An ornament is a decorative embellishment. It is something you put on show to be cherished and admired. But grace is frequently absent from the grace note.

Look at all aspects of the art of the time for extra inspiration. Music and the other arts have always gone hand in hand, continually inspiring each other. Knowledge of contemporary architecture, clothing, dance and history in general can nourish your musical psyche. A particular conundrum is how you should interpret the neo-classical and neo-baroque works of composers like Stravinsky. Do you articulate, ornament and phrase them in the composer's contemporary style, in that of the reflected era, or a little of both?

Another problem we will encounter in musical notation is the bar-line.

The Bar

In performance, the notes frequently appear to be incarcerated behind bars. Playing without bar-lines would in fact be visually confusing: your part would have an endless stream of notes, and offer no trace of phrasing or direction. The dividing up of music into segments gives the performer some useful landmarks. Often the bar-lines do relate to the phrasing. But these vertical lines can lead to vertical playing, and can easily destroy the horizontal flow of the music. Emphasizing the beginning of every bar, or even of every beat, can give the listener motion-sickness. We are taught in the early stages of learning our instrument that we should always play towards the bar-lines. But as we advance it can become a mere habit; and if it is done without thought it can be insulting to the composer and destructive. You wouldn't dream of drawing grid-lines all over the Mona Lisa, and yet you hear the musical equivalent of this day after day. Bar-lines are musical packages that you must unwrap.

CD Culture

With the development of digital technology and the invention of the compact disk, recording companies now have extraordinary techniques at their disposal. They enable them to produce cleaner and more perfect reproductions than ever before. In the recording 'box' they have the facility to pinpoint a single note from one 'take' and place it precisely on top of another one. Producers often re-take sections, cutting and pasting passages as easily and frequently as we do with text on computers, and making them sound flawless on playback. There are several outcomes to this 'perfect recording' culture, the first of which was brought to my attention by my grandfather thirty years ago when he attended 'music appreciation' classes at night-school. The mature students would study a work in the class, following the score and listening to vinyl disks. Afterwards, they all attended a live performance of the work. My grandfather remarked that a few people in the class never enjoyed the concerts as much as the recordings. He recalled that during the performances there would often be a few split notes in the brass, and that perhaps a wrong note would appear in one of the woodwind solos; and he admitted that the strings could sound a little scratchy. He used to laugh about one chap who regularly complained, authoritatively, that the balance was not quite right.

We have become conditioned to expect faultless performances every time we put on a CD. Today's recordings offer us a perfect balance between sections of the orchestra giving us 'crystal-clear' instruments, with individual solos highlighted like decorative gilt-edging. Is it over sanitized, this impeccably luscious sound? It is not surprising, though, that the arm-chair listener with his CD collection, his remote control and a large brandy by his side is often disappointed when attending a live performance in a concert hall.

How Many Takes Does It Take?

The second thing I have noticed in connection with the CD culture is that when music students listen to recordings of eminent musicians, they expect to be able to replicate their playing without taking into account how many years the artist in question has dedicated to performing. It may have taken them as long as twenty or thirty years to become players of their calibre. All the same, students do often become agitated, and hope to reach such elevation in only a fraction of the time.

Musicians are human and even the 'masters' make mistakes. Consider, when listening to recordings, how many re-takes would have been done to produce that note-perfect interpretation, and how much spliced tape must have been left on the cutting-room floor at the end of the recording session.

Study or Mimic

Recordings can be a helpful tool, and an enormous amount can be learnt from studying different players' methods. But be careful. Rather than imitating them mindlessly, analyse and scrutinize their style, attack and unique sound, along with their particular musicality. If you just mimic them, you may end up playing like a clone: a dilute version of the original without the substance and understanding. When you *study* recordings, question the musical conclusions implied in them; experiment with the ideas behind them rather than wholeheartedly adopting them.

Put all these musical thoughts and ideas into a large cooking pot, and remember that your own fundamental beliefs are the *main* ingredient. Over the years and with a bit of luck, an intelligent, innovative musical philosophy should come out, cooked to perfection.

Soul Music

For some indigenous tribes, making a photographic portrait of them meant the capturing and theft of their soul. Often in recording sessions, attention to detail eclipses the desire to capture the atmosphere of the performance. Sometimes musicality, interpretation and flow are sacrificed so that note-perfection can prevail. It is extremely difficult to reproduce the electricity of a live performance within the sterile confines of a recording studio as elements in its character often seem to have gone missing once the music is transferred to a digital signal. I have heard producers remark that a tempo suitable for a concert is not necessarily the right one for a recording, and I have witnessed musicians creating magic only to be disappointed on playback. In an attempt to counteract this, one famous artist only uses notes from complete takes when his recordings are edited, insisting that they sound very different from isolated mini re-takes.

Another factor to consider when doing a recording in a studio is that the musicians know in advance that the flow will be destroyed. Would they play differently if they knew they only had one chance of getting it right? The incessant stopping and starting in a recording session may be partly to blame for creating the wrong atmosphere. If we are not careful, the CD could become for musicians what the camera was for those indigenous people. The soul can too easily be stolen from the music.

Chapter 4

Auditions

'The expression of thought, of sentiment,
of the passions, must be the true aim of music.'
Jean-Philippe Rameau, 1683–1764

One of the biggest hurdles you will encounter when pursuing an orchestral career is the audition. Very few players enjoy the experience. It is an event so harrowing that it can turn the most experienced of players into a quivering lump of jelly even before they can get their instrument out of its case. However, with the exception of a select and lucky few, we all have to do them.

The first thing is to know where to look.

- *In Britain, all orchestral jobs are advertised in the arts section of the Saturday edition of the* Daily Telegraph.
- *Vacancies world-wide can be found in a German publication called* Das Orchester.

It is worth buying *Das Orchester* occasionally to become aware of the pages of orchestral jobs that are available outside the UK.

One method gaining popularity is to use the internet. Recently a couple of web-sites have been set up with pages dedicated to orchestral vacancies. One that I recommend you to visit is:

- *www.musicalchairs.info*

This also has listings of players, instrumental sales, competitions and much more.

If you do apply for a job abroad, you should know that other countries have different audition 'rules'. For example, in America, and also in many other countries, auditions are compulsory and there are no exceptions. The process is usually a very thorough affair, and in a way similar to a competition. A position can be awarded solely on the audition day, whether or not the player has played with the orchestra. I recently had a pupil who auditioned for principal flute of the Athens Opera. He was only in the room for ten minutes, he played like a superstar and he got the job.

Never having played with them before, he was offered a job for life. Some European orchestras line up all the candidates in a gladiatorial-style contest. Each player tries desperately to outshine the others and one by one they are dropped until the strongest contender is found.

Whatever their appointing method, most foreign orchestras will then have a trial period for the appointee of between six months and a year, after which, if the players, the conductor and the management are not entirely happy with him, they will then re-advertise the post. In the larger American orchestras, it has been known to take more than six years to fill a principal vacancy, and I have come across players who have been offered a job on this basis, have relinquished their post, have moved house and have watched from afar as their previous position has been filled, only to be turned down after their year's trial.

In Britain we have a unique system of appointing orchestral musicians, with goal-posts that vary in size and position, together with a pitch that has a definite slant. Sometimes it is against you and sometimes it can tip in your favour. We too have auditions, occasionally involving a series of rounds; although some players may bypass this terrifying stage completely if their playing is known and liked by the orchestra concerned. Successful candidates will then be given trials of anything from a single day to several weeks; and over the following months the more suitable players will be offered lengthier trials, while the unsuitable candidates will receive the standard rejection letter.

You can be fooled by superb solo performing in an audition, only to find out within two minutes of the player's trial that they possess no ensemble qualities whatever. Perhaps they can't follow, or have a sound that is incapable of blending within the section. We will be dealing with such problems later on in the book. But I can say here that it is easy once you play alongside someone to assess whether they will be capable of fitting into your orchestra. What takes time is the thorough trials to ascertain who is the best suited and hence the most appropriate player for the job. Eventually, a player will definitely be chosen, although some orchestras do still have an extra year's 'try out' period as a 'get-out clause'. In Britain, it is rarely used as the initial trials are extensive and cover a wide range of repertoire and styles, and they enable the relevant players to gauge potential, assess merit, spot faults and consider personality clashes, all before the job is offered.

When Should You Start Applying?

The short answer is straight away. As long as you have undertaken formal study, and perform at a standard that reflects your years of training, I recommend that you apply at once as most players need experience in order to get used to the audition format:

> The more auditions I did, the more I got used to the set up and to what to expect.
>
> Victoria Daniel

Clocking up audition experience is the best way of getting used to your nerves, and helps you to find an audition technique that works for you.

> I had nine or ten attempts before I got any extra work at all; I believe there is a real art form in doing auditions that you have to learn.
>
> Peter Dixon

The quicker you can get through those first few – usually catastrophic – attempts and survive, the better.

- *Not all players will be given an audition, and not all jobs are advertised.*

Every orchestra differs in its approach to the question of who will be given an audition and which forms will go straight into the shredding-machine. There are some orchestras that will only consider listening to players with vast experience, and others that will hear almost anybody. Even when an orchestra invites a wide spectrum of candidates to audition, those candidates should be prepared to accept that if one of them is the applicant who only began playing their instrument last Christmas (and this has happened) or else is a rather mature player who has never worked professionally, they will probably be ignored. Rightly or wrongly, the usual cut-off age for applicants with no previous professional orchestral experience will be around thirty-five, and possibly even less. But:

- *If you are a talented student nearing the end of your course, you must apply.*

Don't wait until you are perfect, because you will end up waiting for ever. If you are refused an audition because of lack of experience, you must remain positive and keep banging at the audition door until you are given the chance to prove yourself. If you deserve to succeed, then you will. It is often a matter of time and patience.

> My goal was always to get into an orchestra, so I started auditioning for jobs in my third year at college. I remember many of my contemporaries saying that they didn't feel ready; but you never feel ready. My success rate at the beginning was relatively high because I got trials and extra work straight away. I think being young and an unknown quantity can actually help sometimes. The older you get, the more you have to prove, and also the more you have to lose.
>
> Miriam Skinner

Students

Students will usually be heard for extra work (see 'Auditions for Extra Work' later in this chapter, on page 79), but, as I have mentioned, they can often be ignored for jobs unless they have won international competitions, or have a very good reference from a noted player, or are perhaps known to members of the panel. I consider it unwise for music students to be ignored for full-time jobs. Obviously they will not have much experience but they may have an incredibly advanced technique and also be flexible and receptive. They need real audition experience, and it is short-sighted for orchestras to reject them automatically. It is in their interest to view the 'up-and-coming' talent as potential that may turn out to be the perfect investment for them. I was given my job while still at college. So maybe I'm biased. But when we were appointing my first section member, the management at the time tried to cut down the number of auditions because there were over a hundred applicants. Students were an obvious target for elimination, but one of them had a glorious reference from a celebrated player whom I admired. Without such a testimonial, his form would no doubt have been thrown straight into the bin. Yes, you guessed correctly: that student, who so nearly failed even to get an audition because of his age and status, performed astoundingly well. He was awarded a trial and subsequently got the job. Ever since, I have always made a point of hearing as many people as I am allowed to. You never know which players are going to blossom ... The moral of the story is:

- *Sometimes a good reference from a noted player can be as important as a gold star CV.*

CV Versus Resumé

When you send in your application form, you will have to include details of your career so far. Some people prefer to submit a resumé that is more like a programme-note or a biography than a regular curriculum vitae; but whatever your choice of format, make it clear. Many professional players won't have enough time to study your letter of application carefully before your audition. Therefore, just like the very first note you play, the first sentence of your resumé must grab the panel's attention. If, on the day, your playing is in dire straits while your CV is impressive, it could be a life-saver.

Formal qualifications are not required for playing in a symphony orchestra, but a list of competitions you have won, press-cuttings, and famous players and conductors with whom you have performed can sometimes impress. All the same, what we are fundamentally interested in is *professional orchestral experience*. If you write down your experience chronologically, the more relevant work may be lost among the dross. So:

- *Put important information at the beginning, and make it easy for us to find it.*

The more experience you have, the more impressive your resumé will be. However, there is one thing that is even more important to add, and surprisingly it is frequently forgotten:

- *Put the instrument you play clearly at the top of the form.*

> We get CVs sent to us in the office and quite often we look at them and say: 'What is their instrument?' We have no idea. They may have performed with many orchestras and have vast experience, but that is no good to us if we don't know what instrument they play!
>
> Helena Miles

- *Don't add irrelevant points.*

We recently had someone applying for extra work who told us that he had been awarded three gold stars for his services at a

McDonald's restaurant. Although it might be relevant for other jobs, such information should not appear on your application form for an orchestra. Even if you desperately need to pad out your experience:

- *Don't bore them to death with reams of local news clippings of prizes you have won from the age of eight onwards.*

Music college was absolutely dreadful when describing to you how your CV should look. As a student, I was given a specimen CV and over the years I have realized that virtually all the categories were worthless. Orchestral members just want the appropriate information: they don't need to know which conductors you have worked with, or what master classes you attended, as it is not relevant to them. They want one sheet of paper with your orchestral experience written down, along with any high-quality solo and chamber work, and that is it. If you pad it out with pointless stuff, it is really obvious that you haven't done much. I have seen professional players passing around someone's CV and laughing because it was four pages long and yet only had one orchestral gig on it – they found it comical; and so the colleges should sort this out because they are making the students look foolish. I discovered it the hard way and I now have my CV on one page: the way it should have been from the very beginning. Of course, when you're starting out, you're not going to have any professional experience; but trying to disguise it by telling them that you played in a quintet in your first year is embarrassing and looks desperate. Your college symphony and chamber orchestras would be acceptable, but everything else – leave it out. With that you're doing more harm than good.

Nic Dowton

- *Don't lie.*

When we were holding auditions for a principal position a few years ago, one applicant sent us a most impressive resumé. It caught our attention. He had glorious critiques and comments from famous conductors. He told us that he had performed as a soloist with many professional orchestras, ours included. This worried me since I did not recognize him. I gave him the benefit of the doubt, thinking that perhaps I had not played in that particular concert, or that it had been before my time. When he started playing, we were troubled. He wasn't terribly good; in fact *terrible* was the word! Finally, our leader noticed that one of the comments in his resumé was by an illustrious conductor who had died before the candidate was born. Don't lie. Your playing will always tell the truth.

The Audition Loophole – Back Door

At the discretion of each organization, some players may not be required to audition and will be given orchestral trials straight away. These lucky players may include people who are already in jobs in other orchestras or are well-known freelancers. Doing without auditions may seem unfair, but for some they are unnecessary. As I have said, we have extensive trial periods in this country: they are thorough and it usually takes about a year to fill a post.

This does, however, create an anomaly in the audition process since it is possible, in theory, to become a professional player without ever having succeeded in an audition. Being in the right place at the right time is a big factor. When a contract player is ill and all the usual 'extra players' are unavailable, *you* may receive a phone call – provided that you have sent in your details.

- *Make contact with all your local orchestras and give them your phone number.*

Sometimes in an emergency and out of desperation, when they are unable to consult any of the contract players, orchestral fixers have to phone up and hire totally unknown players.

It is worth adding that if you are hired under such circumstances, you should not relate the gratitude of the surrounding players to your standard of performance that evening. In an emergency, everyone will be eternally grateful that you are just sitting in the correct chair so that there isn't a gap on the stage, and the fact that you can actually play your instrument is a real bonus.

In reality,

- *You have to do a fantastic job to make an impression.*

This doesn't mean playing louder than everyone else, although many newcomers do fall into this trap. The chapters that follow will help you to make a positive impression by enriching your ensemble playing, improving your intonation and giving you networking ideas and survival tips. Read on, succeed through the audition process, and then:

- *Prove yourself to be the 'perfect extra player', since more work will come your way.*

Good extra players are worth their weight in gold, and:

- *Principal players in each orchestra keep a close eye on who is being hired by the other bands.*

Having a good reputation and getting known is all part of the game. A worthy player's name will travel effortlessly through the profession. In time it may lead to him stepping up the rungs of the audition ladder and being offered trials.

- *Once you have done a trial in a professional orchestra, many other doors will open, even if you don't get the job.*

Students don't realize that professional players listen all the time and communicate with each other. Orchestral management, players, critics and music agents are often invited to music-college concerts and may be out there listening to you. So remember:

- *You are always on show.*

The Audition

After music college, one of the first encounters you will have with professional musicians will be at your orchestral audition. If you have participated regularly in mock auditions at college, you will find there is *no* similarity between them. If you think that you have conquered your nerves for performing, think again. Professional orchestral auditions are for real. They matter, and when you audition for the first time, you will probably be overcome by nerves.

To be forewarned is to be forearmed. By giving you knowledge of what goes on behind the audition-room door, I hope I can prepare you in advance.

Let us first look at:

The Panel

The panel will be made up of members of the orchestra. Often there will be a representative from the management; the conductor will occasionally be an observer; and there will definitely be at least one specialist in your instrument. Beware. You may not see any of them because they may be – invisible (behind a screen).

This is more common in North America, but it sometimes happens here as well. If you have not encountered it before, it may be worthwhile for you to enquire beforehand whether the auditions are screened so that you can prepare yourself. It is a very different experience playing to a curtain. You will be given a number, and you may be disqualified for saying anything in such a blind round. The panel must not be able to identify you, or determine your age, race or sex. I did hear of a bizarre screened audition a few years ago, though, when a colleague told me that she had to walk into a room in full view of the panel before positioning herself behind a screen, where her legs were still showing. Obviously no one had told them that in a screened audition it is easier to make the panel invisible than the applicant, who needs access into and out of the room.

There are a couple more screened-audition stories I feel are worth sharing. First, there was a player who did a shockingly bad audition. He must have guessed that he hadn't got through the round, so he decided to say something. He went up to the screen and whispered to the panel: 'Forgive me, father, for I have sinned!'

Another well circulated, modern allegorical tale, which has more serious undertones, illustrates that while screened auditions may seem fair on the outside, everyone can make mistakes, which may result in the best players sometimes not even getting through the first round. A newly appointed trumpet-player in a major US orchestra was asked to sit on the panel to appoint a successor for his former position. The auditions were screened and the only requirement for getting through the first round was not to miss a single note. Candidates came in, slipped up and were told to go home. As a result, the panel had got ahead of schedule. Out of pure mischievousness, this particular panellist excused himself and instructed them to carry on without him for a few minutes. Unknown to them, he nipped round to the front, grabbed his trumpet and auditioned, and after a few minutes he heard the panel say 'Thank you, that will be all.' He had lost his own job because he was not good enough.

If the audition is not screened, you will be able to see the panel. But don't be surprised if they look – bored and not in the slightest bit interested.

You hear stories of candidates travelling two hundred miles only to have the panel talk all the way through their audition. I know someone who got fed up with this, said 'sorry to bother you' and walked out.

Miriam Skinner

I have been on panels with eight or nine players, and you can expect to see more. A long row of unknown faces, some smiling, some looking bored out of their minds: expect them all! Whether they convey a formal or an informal atmosphere, the panel should attempt to make you feel welcome so that you can show them your full capability.

> I have had the privilege of sitting in on an audition to listen, and I realized that it can be a positive atmosphere. I found that I was willing people to play well. I really wanted them to do their best.
>
> Miriam Skinner

However, you will occasionally find that there are panellists who will be condescending towards you and deliberately make you feel inadequate. I'm sorry, that's life. There are unsavoury characters around. Be prepared to encounter them either at your audition or at some point later on in your career.

- *Don't be distracted by conversation or movement among members of the panel.*

They need to be able to talk to each other, and I have known people to talk on purpose in order to see whether the candidate was easily distracted.

From the moment you enter the audition room, try to be yourself both as individual and as player.

- *Try to enjoy yourself.*

If you don't enjoy your playing, the panel won't either. They may have heard your concerto played a hundred times in the last three days. It is no wonder that they may look bored when you enter the room.

- *Never feel insulted by this. Instead seize the opportunity and make it your duty to wake them up. Play your heart out and mesmerize them.*

> I always play at auditions as if I were performing in a solo recital.
>
> Fiona Cross

Sometimes the panel can be:

the whole section, or even the whole orchestra.

It is not that common in Britain, but you may be auditioning on the Continent where this is a regular occurrence. In my orchestra, for instance, the whole 'cello section has been asked to observe at auditions, and the Liverpool Philharmonic often invite the whole orchestra to attend auditions for principal positions. They don't all show up; but imagine how you would feel entering a room expecting three or four people only to be confronted by the whole band. Be prepared for anything. It may be wise to find out who is on the panel just before you enter, so that the paramedics don't have to be called in to resuscitate you.

How Long Will I Be in There?

Ten minutes is average for an extra-work audition, and fifteen to twenty minutes for a permanent post. But beware of:

the four-minute audition

- *Don't try to read anything into how long you were in an audition.*

There is no such equation as, 'the length of time you are in an audition is proportional to the probability of your getting into the next round.' One regularly overhears players coming out saying: 'They must have liked me because I was in there for almost twenty minutes.' This may be true, but I have been in a position where I have been told to allocate twenty minutes to every candidate regardless of their standard. In this situation, hearing a complete work through to the end can be a real time-waster. If you are good, we'll know about it within minutes, if not seconds. At times, we can tell how someone is going to play from their body language as they walk into the room. Sometimes we are wrong, but not often.

Musicality is totally subjective and we all have different tastes in sounds and styles. However, as I say:

- *We should be able to tell within seconds whether the candidate is up to standard, and if they are, it only takes another four minutes to see whether we are interested in them for a trial.*

If you think this attitude is off-hand or flippant, and only relates to the performing arts, consider the following data from a recent survey of business interviews: 90% of decisions as to whether the interviewee would or would not get the job, were made within the first thirty seconds of their entering the room.

When you receive your audition time and date, you will also be told what to prepare. A standard audition format will follow this pattern:

Two contrasting works – often one of these will be set by the orchestra.
Orchestral excerpts.
Sight-reading.

What Are We Looking For in an Audition?

> You do still tend to get a fair few for whom one might say that the audition was misguided: they just don't seem to understand the basic level of playing technique that you require to even start.
>
> Robert Chasey

When I interviewed the principal 'cellist Peter Dixon, I asked him what it was he looked for in a candidate applying for work, and to illustrate the commonest mistakes for me.

> For my auditions, I always keep a set format by asking applicants to play a couple of pieces of their own choice. I don't see the point of imposing a piece on them as I think people should feel comfortable with whatever style of music they want to play. The main thing I'm looking for is the sound. If they haven't got the sound, then it doesn't matter how good they are: I'm not interested. Personally, I'm looking for sound that will blend with the whole section. I like to appoint players who make a big sound but not a harsh one, because I find that you can always turn a big sound down but it's very hard to turn a small sound up. So I go for the big players who are going to conform, and that is obviously something you find out about when they actually get a trial. 30% of applicants are usually nowhere near the required standard so I have to discover the really good players among the remaining 70%.
>
> Orchestral excerpts prove to be a problem for an alarming number of candidates. It really distresses me when someone has played the Dvořák concerto beautifully, and then you give them a very basic piece

of orchestral repertoire – that they have actually been given in advance – and they ask you questions like 'How fast does this go?' That to me is an absolute *no no*. I do tend to set unusual repertoire, but I make sure that the office will have sent the music to them at least a month in advance. A couple of appointments ago, we were recording Hindemith's symphony in Eb and there was a very difficult section for the 'cellos in triplets, and the metre was quite clearly given at the beginning of the movement. It was unbelievable: I would say 85% of the people played it at the wrong speed; and that is worrying because it shows a real lack of care.

A particular gripe I have is when people play dotted rhythms as triplets. That sort of thing happens all the time and is a mistake. If they are obviously very talented, I would be prepared to say: 'Hey look, do you know you're going ♪♪ ♪♪ rather than ♪♪ ♪♪,' and often they may get it right once or twice before going off into triplets again. That is no good to me because they've got to be a team-player. They can't just go wandering off on their own.

Peter Dixon

Orchestral Excerpts

• *I cannot overemphasize the importance of learning orchestral excerpts.*

The matter of sight-reading and excerpt-learning also came up quickly when I asked Jonathan Goodall, our principal horn player for thirty-one years, what *he* looked for in auditions and what he too considered were the commonest mistakes.

I look for a combination of things: a good sound, good intonation and secure rhythm. They definitely need to be accurate in getting the notes right, and these days it is very important to have good reading ability because there isn't much rehearsal time. My teacher laid a lot of emphasis on knowing the repertoire well; and so in auditions, I would definitely hear some standard excerpts that they really should know, along with an element of pure sight-reading, just to see how they cope.

Some players are really 'clued up' in auditions: you can tell that they have done the work. Others, however, think that it's OK just to come in and play their piece well. If you were to give them Strauss's *Don Juan* and they played the big tune at the wrong speed, that would be totally unacceptable. Recently, many candidates got the tempi all wrong in some standard Brahms. It was surprising because they all have ample opportunity to listen and learn.

Jonathan Goodall

At college I was not made aware of the importance of studying orchestral passages, and I was extremely lucky to get a job without knowing much repertoire. But we cannot all rely on luck. At the audition for my job, after I'd played my pieces and a few prepared excerpts (which I had learned), the distinguished flute player Peter Lloyd said: 'Play us the big flute solo from Brahms's First Symphony.' I replied: '... Um what note does it start on?' He said that it began on a high E. Cheekily, I played a short E and asked: 'Then what?' This was appalling, and I now make sure my own students have a much greater knowledge than I did at that age.

There are some teachers who recommend learning an instrument at music college exclusively through the study of excerpts. While the orchestral repertoire does contain some of the most difficult passages imaginable, this approach goes too far in the opposite direction. The grounding techniques that are required for you to master an instrument will not always be evenly spread within the orchestral repertoire. Possibly some fundamental techniques will be neglected. You need to attain that gorgeous ethereal sound, that immaculate rhythm, that superior technique and that crisp, clear articulation I speak of in the foreword. In addition, you need the ability to identify and sort out problems when things go wrong. A careful balance thus needs to be achieved between studying fundamentals and repertoire. It is only since I have been an orchestral player and sat on audition panels that I have understood the real significance and importance of excerpt learning. I have played all the excerpts in their context, and so I see the relevant orchestral colours in my mind during each section, and imagine how I should blend with the other instruments. For example, as a flautist, I would aim to produce a different sound when playing in unison with a horn from the one I would use when playing with an oboe. I would try a completely different articulation when playing a phrase alongside a clarinet rather than with pizzicato strings. (Colour changes are described in the harmonics section of the *Intonation* chapter (page 158), and articulation and blending are discussed in the *Ensemble* chapter.)

You will find that some excerpts are solos that must penetrate through the texture at all costs, while others must float effortlessly above the whole orchestra. Perhaps one excerpt should possess a strong colour but should remain within the fabric of the music, whereas another should blend invisibly. And then there are excerpts that metamorphose from one thing to another. Getting them the wrong way round will show up like a flashing neon sign that reads 'No Experience Here'. Understanding the repertoire in such depth is the result of playing in a professional orchestra for around twenty years. However, don't be disheartened:

• *Listen to the works.*

With excerpt learning, the part you are studying is only a fraction of the complete work, a brush-stroke from the painted canvas. Stand back to see the whole picture and appreciate its full glory.

• *Study different interpretations of the same work.*

You will find that there are many correct ways of playing each piece. Hearing diverse interpretations of a work played with different tempo, expression and balance will help you discover a mean for audition purposes, as well as giving you an idea of the infinite musical possibilities there are.

• *Go to live performances.*

During recordings, if the balance isn't quite right, the producer or conductor may ask some of the musicians to change their dynamics; and one often finds that engineers 'help' players by turning the microphone levels up and down constantly throughout sessions. This is very convenient from our side of the recording cubicle. However, it can breed laziness, and occasionally the technicians overcompensate. That may lead to a distortion of the natural balance and blending. We will spend years learning to project, blend and hide, only to have it all electronically changed at the flick of a switch. You can hear recordings with an unnatural balance in which players are so closely 'miked' that their line of the music is blown out of musical context, right down your ear.

In 1932, the conductor Leopold Stokowski was outraged when he heard of the existence of sound engineers. Touring NBC's Fifth Avenue studios shortly before commencing a radio series, he observed a man in front of a sound-control panel manipulating a row of dials.

> ''Who is that?' Stokowski asked.
> 'He's the engineer who controls the sound.'
> 'Do you propose to have one on *my* programmes?' Stokowski demanded.
> 'Oh, yes. He's necessary on all programmes.'

'Not on mine. No one controls Stokowski's sounds but Stokowski.' And he marched off.

This put NBC into a real quandary. They patiently explained the facts of broadcasting to Stokowski but to no avail.

He remained adamant. Faced with a crisis, they gave in and reluctantly built at huge cost a portable glass-enclosed control room on rollers for him to operate.

As Stokowski rehearsed, he practised on the dials while the programme staff suffered. He would wave his hands and then suddenly reach down to twist a knob, often the wrong way and invariably too much or too little, for he was unable to gauge the blended sounds as heard in the control room.

Inevitably, the first broadcast was a sonic disaster.

For the next broadcast a bright engineer had an inspiration. 'Let's use *two* control cubicles,' he suggested, 'a well-screened functioning one, and a disconnected play-toy for the conductor.' They built another, and the scheme worked just fine.

No one knows who tipped off Stokowski, but about the third rehearsal he strode right past the glass monster and never looked at it again.'

From *Leopold Stokowski: A Profile* by Abram Chasins
(copyright © 1979 Abram Chasins. Reproduced by kind
permission of: Dutton, a division of Penguin Group
(USA) Inc, and Robert Hale Ltd)

You can never be sure how much distortion in balance has taken place in the recording studio; but when attending live performances you will hear a balance that is closer to what the composer intended.

> I think that you should go to lots of concerts to begin to understand what is needed, although I have found that students don't go to that many live performances, and if they can't get free tickets, they definitely won't go!
>
> Ben Hudson

If you are a non-musician, you may be surprised to hear that music students do not go to many orchestral concerts. If you *are* a music student, then either you will be disagreeing with this or else feeling a little hot under the collar. However, the sheer volume of applicants either for extra work or for full-time vacancies who turn up to auditions with no knowledge whatever of particular set excerpts is astonishing. Even the speeds seem a well-guarded mystery to them. Let me reiterate: these are not the sight-reading passages but the prepared works which we have *told* them we will be hearing.

> Audition excerpts are nearly always the same each time; so have them learnt and regularly practised.
>
> Ben Hudson

- *You should know the tempo of all the excerpts, and the style in which they should be played, as well as being aware of what is going on at any point in the music.*

Getting the notes right and choosing the correct speed is the first step in presenting your orchestral excerpts. Understanding the emotional context of each extract sets the relevant scene. Be conscious of which section of the orchestra is accompanying you during a particular solo, and be aware also of the instrument, or instruments, to which you will be handing over your phrase.

- *Don't insult us: you cannot bluff your way through the excerpts.*

Playing Shostakovich's Ninth Symphony at half speed is as insulting to us as playing the Lithuanian National Anthem at half speed to a Lithuanian audience – which we have done.

Assuming that you have learnt the excerpts in the manner described,

- *Concentrate, and focus on each excerpt you play.*

Hear the orchestra in your head before you start, and continue to do so whilst you are playing: this will help you to relax, choose a good speed and play in a correct style.

- *Be prepared to play an excerpt again in a different manner from what you are accustomed to.*

Even if I love the way a candidate has just played, I often ask them to try a different approach in style and tempo to see whether they are *flexible*.

What Do You Do with the Bars' Rest?

If the excerpt you are playing has some bars' rest in your part, you are not expected to count the bars in an embarrassing silence. You must use your discretion: for a small number of bars, count them; and for a large number, it is perfectly acceptable for you to skip ahead, with one proviso. You must have a couple of seconds' pause before you skip to prepare everyone for the musical leap. Without this, people with a sensitive musical disposition will be unnerved by the distortion in the rhythmical flow.

In addition to the set excerpts, you will probably be given some sight-reading. This may be from the standard orchestral repertoire; and so it may be the luck of the draw whether you have come across the music before. In time, your knowledge will increase, but you can, as a sight-reading precaution:

- *Find out about the repertoire the orchestra is currently performing and rehearsing over the next couple of weeks.*

Quite often the principals will go to their folder in the library and take out the 'music of the week', and use it for sight-reading. But they may deliberately seek out an obscure work that will be new to everyone, too.

Sight-Reading

If you really don't know the work, don't plunge straight into it. Spend a few seconds scanning the passage you're given, and search for potential pitfalls.

- *Work out any complex rhythmical patterns, and perhaps finger out tricky-looking passages.*
- *Check the key signature, dynamics and phrasing.*

As long as you do this within fifteen seconds or so, you won't be marked down. And yet taking the extra time will reap great benefits.

- *If you have no idea of the tempo, ask what it is.*

And you must:

- *Try to keep the pulse going throughout the excerpt.*

The pulse is often more important than playing all the correct notes. With a little practice, anyone can learn the right notes; but not everyone can keep a steady beat. Skipping beats in an audition can be an indication of a much bigger problem that may be difficult to rectify (see 'Rhythm' in the *Ensemble* chapter, on page 96).

- *Don't stop in mid phrase to correct mistakes.*

We can tell whether you are really sight-reading and will adjust our marks accordingly.

- *Try to play musically while sight-reading.*

Artistic sight-reading with a flowing pulse and a few wrong notes is preferable to producing all the correct notes without feeling, as I have said.

Replicate this sight-reading scenario in your practice, and set yourself new material to read every day.

The Truth About Sight-Reading in the Profession

In Britain, we are known and respected for our sight-reading ability, and we are indeed very quick and flexible in our music-making. Foreign conductors visiting British orchestras for the first time are often amazed that the standard of an initial rehearsal can be close to that of a performance, rather than just a 'read through'. Is this due to our sight-reading skills, or are we simply well prepared and adaptable musicians?

Experienced orchestral players will know much of the repertoire in advance, but they will still have to prepare. Some of them may take the music home to browse through. Others may know the important passages so well that they can practise them from memory. There is no magic to sight-reading. The true art of performing is ensemble playing (see the next chapter) and not just playing the right notes at the correct time ... although that happens to be a good starting point. I have seen players come into the rehearsal room early, slip their parts back into their folders and look around furtively to see whether anyone has noticed – obviously they were too proud to admit they needed to practise.

In reality, I have only had to sight-read properly once in public, and that was when the wonderful, legendary pianist John Ogden travelled to the wrong concert hall, in a different town. We were told he would be able to get to us in time for the performance, and we waited for him until the audience were in their seats. But he never arrived. We strode onto the platform that night not knowing what the second item would be. Orchestras usually have some extra works in their library trunker, and one of these was passed around the stage. It was a piece the orchestra knew well, but, being relatively inexperienced, I had never heard it. Quickly scanning the music, I didn't notice anything too technical. But I didn't know which passages were exposed; I had no idea which instruments I was going to be playing with at any point; and I certainly wasn't familiar with the style. I had to alert all my senses and concentrate. Several players, relishing my predicament, lent over my music stand and said: 'Good luck with that tricky solo cadenza' – which in fact didn't exist.

Having to sight-read in a concert is very rare indeed. Even during most emergencies, you will still have the rehearsal to learn the music in and the tea-breaks to conquer any awkward sections. When you record music for television, film and radio, however, having to sight-read is commonplace. Composers for such sessions are notorious for running right up to the deadline and arriving with the music on the day. You will gradually get used to such added extra pressures, and take them in your stride. But for the majority of orchestral concerts:
• *The music is available for you to borrow.*
Don't be embarrassed to ask for it. It may not look cool, but it is always better to be prepared.

Speaking to the oboist Emma Ringrose, I asked her what sort of preparation she did before her first professional orchestral rehearsal.

> I got recordings out of the pieces that I was going to play – I hate not having heard a piece for a concert; and I also rang up the orchestra's librarian and got them to send me the music. I think it is always good to do that, and you have to know the part because everyone else will.
> Emma Ringrose

• *If it is not possible to get the music, then go to a music department in a large library and take the scores out.*

As a serious orchestral contender, you must also:
• *Buy the orchestral excerpt books for your instrument.*
There are volumes of these excerpt books that are available for sale, and they will contain all the major solos and exposed passages for your instrument as well as many other difficult sections you may come across in your career. When studying these, you must not just learn the solos or the upper lines, but you must look at the less glamorous parts as well. Many students make this mistake, only to find that, when they do get professional work, it will probably be those secondary lines they will be asked to play.

Although the excerpt books are an essential aid, you must be aware that many of them are riddled with errors. These may confuse you and put you off when you play from the real parts during your audition. Every time a pupil comes to me for an orchestral lesson, I find I am continually changing phrasing, correcting articulation and adding accidentals that are missing from such publications. And so it would be worth your while playing through the relevant passages with an experienced orchestral player: not only for reasons of style but also so that such corrections can be made. Playing from the real parts can be confusing for other reasons as well:

> I made a mistake in one solo purely because the music in the excerpt book was written on one page, while in the audition I was reading the manuscript, where the solo was split over two. I should have known it from memory, but being nervous, the visual difference really stumped me.
>
> Linda Verrier

In an attempt to counteract these problems, many British orchestras now send each candidate a booklet containing all the required excerpts (minus any sight-reading). However, I have noticed that occasionally these publications are merely photocopies of excerpt books (still containing errors) rather than copies of the sheet music we read as orchestral musicians.

Audition Nerves

> You never know how you are going to play on the day. I find that I can still do bad auditions, even though the one before may have gone really well and I may have gone away feeling that I had nailed auditions once and for all. From experience you learn how you are going to react, and where the nerves are going to take you.
>
> Nic Dowton

There is a whole chapter later on that is devoted to performance nerves (see page 112) but I felt that, for most players, the nerves they will experience in auditions are likely to be much worse and need special attention.

In an audition, you are under extra pressure as the direction of your whole career may depend on your proving your worth within a few minutes. Your senses are heightened; your emotions and fears exaggerated:

I was on the train going to the audition, and I managed to convince myself that it was going to be disastrous from the start. It was an audition that was primarily on a subsidiary instrument to my own; and having only had seven days' notice, I hadn't spent enough time practising. [See the note on 'Subsidiary Instruments' later in this chapter (page 79) as well as the 'Practice' section in the *Nerves* chapter, on page 114.]

AC

• *We know that all candidates will be nervous about auditions.* Nerves can reveal themselves in many different ways. Some candidates may come in shaking like a leaf and yet sound fantastic, while others may appear arrogant or aloof but be unable to play because of the stress.

Time seems to go by at a different speed when you are nervous. Sometimes a candidate will move rather fast and make exaggerated movements; another will appear to move in slow motion. You may have witnessed both types of symptom when watching young performers: they will either race onto the stage, hurriedly bow to the public and then begin playing immediately; or else they will simply freeze. At the advanced stage of auditioning for a professional symphony orchestra, such symptoms won't be so marked, but if you know which group you belong to, you can plan to counteract the problem.

Another sign of nerves is that people say silly things: auditions are no exception in this respect. Many people come in and start talking inanely about the air-conditioning in their hotel room, or exclaim vociferously how nervous they are. So do heed this advice:

Do not chat too much with the panel.

Fiona Cross

Joking with the panel is also a mistake, although an experienced panellist should be able to see beyond such nervous gaffes.

• *We accept and expect some slips due to nerves.*

We really ought to try and make you feel as comfortable as possible so that you can play at your best; but, as I have said, there are panellists around who love to make candidates sweat, perhaps because the applicant in question is good, or perhaps because they are bad. If a panellist appears malicious or demanding, though, it may be his or her intention to stretch your abilities to their limits.

- *We all want the best player to get the job and if we can induce you to play at your best, our perception of you will be more accurate.*

> My way of getting over audition nerves is to give myself a little pep talk: I tell myself that I know I can play well, and to just go for it!
>
> Nic Dowton

- *If you do make a slip, don't then kamikaze the rest of the audition.*

A performance is not like a driving test where, if you make a mistake, you know that you will automatically have failed. When you make an error while playing in an audition, you can recover from it. If you do so seamlessly, it can be a point in your favour.

> I think people are more forgiving in the UK as they want to see what you *can* do rather than applying the 'one mistake and you're out' method they adopt in some countries. If you make a slip in an audition and you have the confidence to do so, I believe that you can redeem yourself.
>
> Ben Hudson

- *Never show your frustration or anger when you make a mistake.*

Candidates will often be so nervous they won't know themselves, and they may blow up their faults or fears in their minds.

- *Whatever happens, keep going!*

As I have said, it is good to get the first couple of auditions out of the way while you are under the protection and security of your music college. You can experience the levels of stress that will be involved and learn to find a 'coping mechanism' to deal with your nerves before entering the big wide world. As your audition experience increases, you will become familiar with how your nerves show themselves, and this will allow you to prepare yourself mentally and emotionally. You should see a rapid improvement during your first few audition attempts as you familiarize yourself with the procedures and begin to develop an audition technique that will work for you.

> I did a few auditions in my last year of music college. The first one was disastrous, and afterwards I went back to my flat thinking that I would never be able to get any work with those sorts of nerves: I could play the notes but I couldn't control my embouchure I was shaking so

much. I'm glad I forced myself to do another audition soon after as there was a big difference between them. I felt that I had improved.

Victoria Daniel

Most auditions will be in a large room, sometimes even in a concert hall. Not only can its cavernous size be overwhelming but your tone may sound and feel very different in such an acoustic. This can throw your concentration. So:

- *Play a couple of notes to see how your instrument responds in the acoustic before you start performing.*
- *Occasionally practise in a large room.*

With experimentation and practice, you will learn to adjust immediately and sound good in all acoustics. Many young players seek out the most resonant room in their house so that they can achieve the very best sound with the least amount of effort. A drier acoustic, though less flattering, will allow you to hear yourself more clearly as there will be less reverberation. You will have to work harder on your tone since any defects will be highlighted. But there is an advantage: any other room you subsequently play in will immediately make you feel wonderful by comparison.

We have talked about the nerves you will encounter during auditions, and we have seen how becoming stressed can unbalance you on your way to the audition. But there is another challenge to face as well.

The Warm-Up Room

This is a place where men and women can turn into human blanc-manges within seconds of entering. It is the psychic fighting arena where neuroses, conspiracy, intrigue and rumour are rampant. On the audition circuit, you will sometimes be given a communal room, either to warm up in, or just to wait in before you play through your solo works with the official accompanist. If you are lucky, your wait may be fairly brief; but forty minutes of sitting with the enemy may set off paranoia, and cause the most confident musician's heart-beat to race!

> I was put into a room which was shared with two other people. I hate sharing dressing-rooms because you all have to warm up at the same time. There were sight-reading excerpts in the room to practise, but I didn't want to play them in front of the others and make a fool of

myself. The other two seemed really relaxed and in control. I was
totally intimidated by them and started shaking like a leaf.

AC

You may begin to recognize some of the opposition. There may be
some friends from your college, and there will definitely be
strangers as well. All will want the job for themselves, and some
of them will make intimidating remarks such as: 'Oh I thought
you'd given up years ago', or 'I didn't know anyone still played
on that make of instrument.' Other classics include, 'You studied
with whom?' and an old favourite aimed at the jugular: 'Of course
I've been their no.1 freelance player for years now. But good luck
anyway, and enjoy the experience.'
• *Everyone sounds good behind a closed door.*
As you leave the warm-up room and head towards your audition,
beware of something that I call the 'door-filter'. Acoustical engineers and concert-hall architects should harness the physical qualities of doors and use them to produce better concert halls. For no
matter what the standard of the performance behind a closed
door, the sound on the other side will be absolutely marvellous.

> By the time I had to walk into the audition, my legs were going
> absolutely crazy. It was a nightmare! I chose to play an unaccompanied
> piece to start with, so I didn't have to worry about playing with piano,
> and that allowed me to start relaxing. It seemed to be going OK after
> all.
>
> AC

• *Choose your pieces wisely.*
Choosing a solo piece coupled with an accompanied one may
seem a good idea, and it will save rehearsal time with the official
pianist; but I would recommend you to play such a solo very
accurately indeed since alarm bells tend to go off. The panel will
ask why this person has chosen to play without the piano. Can
they play in time? Can they play in tune with the piano? How are
their 'ensemble ears'? Doubts can also arise when players bring
modern 'squeaky-gate' works to an audition. These can sound
quite remarkable, but they may mask the qualities we are seeking.
I was taking a master-class in Greece a few years ago, and a player
gave an amazing performance of a composition of his own for
solo flute that riveted the whole class. It included chords, glissandi

and other astonishing effects, but such alarm bells did start to sound. After the clapping had died down, I asked him if he had anything else to perform and he offered us a Mozart concerto, minus the piano part. Fortunately, I happened to be carrying a copy, and I insisted that he played the piece with the accompaniment. The result was unbelievable. He could not play two bars remotely in time and had no concept of basic rhythm. His ensemble abilities were non-existent, and he couldn't even produce a reasonable tone for more than a split second. I believe that classical musicians should be trained formally so that they can play with a beautiful sound and master their instrument in many styles before they embark on experimental music of this nature. You would think that that would be common practice throughout the art world. However, an artist recently told me that some students attending art college had been told to conceptualize abstract art before commencing their rudimentary training. In her day she studied many of the Great Masters' techniques, re-creating the works of Turner, Degas and Morandi for example, examining their brush strokes and analysing their style, before attempting to find a medium that suited her. There are links here with my thoughts on essential study that are set out in the *Performing Philosophies* chapter.

> 'Technique is to be able to lay open the basic sense of a great work of art, to make it clear.'
> Eugene Istomin, 1925–2003,
> American pianist

> There is a solo piece by Stravinsky that I play for all auditions, I know it very well and feel comfortable performing it. I seldom play Brahms as the piano part is very difficult and needs a lot of rehearsal time: also, you never know the standard of the pianist you're going to get.
> Fiona Cross

Choosing your pieces for an audition is extremely important. The right one will show off what you can do, impress the panel and make them smile. The wrong one will make their shoulders slump in disappointment. Ironically, candidates often choose works that highlight their faults with startling clarity.

Let us now return to the audition itself.

I was coping but then, in an excerpt, I split a note and I thought: that was an easy bit. If I messed that up, what were the next ones going to be like – which were much more difficult? I knew they were going to be disastrous, and they were.

AC

At this point in the audition, the candidate's thoughts had sabotaged his ability to play well. He had not practised enough, and he knew it. Sharing a warm-up room would have begun to wear away his remaining confidence, and in the audition any blunder would probably have finished him off completely. You have to be strong-willed at all times to counter such mind-games. (There is much additional advice on coping with nerves in the *Nerves* chapter, as I have said.)

> In the last excerpt, I didn't even know the piece. I had seen it in the excerpt books but hadn't learnt it, and I actually stopped whilst playing. They asked me if I wanted to have another go, and I just knew there was no point because I was totally finished. I should have walked out. This was the worst audition ever: it was so humiliating. Previously, I have auditioned well and been awarded trials for principal positions; and yet this was only an audition for extra work. On the positive side, though, it was a good lesson for me since I now practise that subsidiary instrument a lot more.

AC

This player hasn't suffered from his experience, and is a very successful freelancer. It is sometimes good to have lessons like this so long as you can:

• *Learn from your mistakes.*

Rumours

You will hear rumours of players being offered the job in advance of your audition, and this will play havoc with your nerves. An orchestra may in fact be keeping a player in mind. But this will probably be their 'insurance policy'. Who can blame them for wanting to ensure that they maintain their standards or even improve on them? A job which has not been signed and sealed is not a *fait accompli*. What is more, they haven't heard *you* playing yet.

Auditions for Extra Work

As I have mentioned, auditions are not always for a full-time position. All orchestras have 'extra-work' lists that are constantly being updated. These cater for situations when some of the contract players are ill, or playing with other bands, or when the repertoire requires 'extra players'. For example, all the Mahler symphonies need extra wind, brass and percussion players since he wrote for a larger-than-average orchestra. Also, because of the large number of string players there are in an orchestra, extra string players are almost always required as there is frequently someone off sick.

> I auditioned for 'extra work' at the beginning of my fourth year, and I was put on a list. It just happened that the orchestra needed a player at the last minute and no one else was available.
>
> Nic Dowton

To get on these lists you must write to the orchestral manager and request an audition. Such auditions can range from being informal (just the principal player in an odd lunch break, without an official accompanist) to being a regular six-monthly event with the atmosphere of a formal audition. In the *Surviving in the Orchestral Profession* chapter, we will observe that it can take orchestras up to a year to hear applicants for 'extra-work' – so write to them now.

Subsidiary Instruments

- *Always take your piccolo/Eb clarinet/cor anglais, etc., with you for an extra-work audition.*

If you are a wind-player seeking extra work, you are expected to be fluent on the whole array of instruments within the family of your particular instrument. It amazes me as a flute player how many potential extra flautists turn up at auditions without a piccolo. I feel they are under the impression that, if successful, they would be asked to play principal. Unless you are extremely lucky, most of your initial extra work will be playing 'down the line' on your main instrument, or filling in on a subsidiary one. All orchestras have a built-in infrastructure for the 'stepping up' of players within the section, or for the hiring of principals from other orchestras when the occasion arises.

We have looked at the process of selecting musicians during auditions. As we near the end of this chapter, let us look at a few additional points before and after the event.

Pre-Audition

I have heard this so many times from students and colleagues: 'I'm not ready yet', or 'If I play badly now, they will remember me in the future.' One rarely feels ready, and as an overworked panel we are unlikely to remember your playing in a year from now, although we might just remember your face, which could be a positive thing. Yes, of course, make sure you are playing well. But:
• *Don't cancel on the day simply because your nerves are telling you that you are not quite ready.*
Many people cancel on the day, probably because of such worries. Even worse, in every set of auditions I have taken, there have always been several candidates who haven't shown up. Without the courtesy of contact from you, we will be left twiddling our thumbs.

If you are thinking about what to wear for your audition, you should:
• *Dress reasonably smartly.*
I remember a cowboy who came to his audition wearing a cape and a ten-gallon hat. I know standards change continually; but if you come in with split jeans and Wellington boots it will show a lack of respect. If you play like an angel, you will succeed whatever happens; however, if you desire to become an orchestral member, you will have to conform to some sort of dress code eventually. Why not start now for your audition?

If you are out of work and in between auditions, you may find it difficult to keep up your standards. Consider:
• *Taking lessons with players.*
These may have multiple benefits. Not only will the occasional lesson give you direction and motivation but taking them could lead to your getting some work. Having a lesson with a respected principal player will be an audition in its own right, and is a commonplace occurrence. Players' phone numbers are to be found

in the Musicians' Union directory. Ring up the player of your choice and ask them whether they have time to give you an advice lesson. Some players are happy to do this. Others feel strongly that they can only give tuition over an extended period rather than as a one-off encounter. Probe the views of the player during your lesson, and listen to their professional judgment.

- *It is the principals of the orchestra who choose their extra-work lists and so decide on tomorrow's orchestral players.*

I have on several occasions run out of players on my extra-work list at 7.30 on the morning of a recording and, because of the short notice, have turned to my teaching phone-book.

Post-Audition

After each audition, you need to 'self-assess'. Although a few people will succeed in getting trials, all candidates except one will eventually receive rejection letters.

> You have to be positive and not consider getting the job as the only way to measure your progress. Just playing well or getting through the round should be considered a success, and being awarded a trial should be deemed a great achievement.
>
> Fiona Cross

> I also count it as a success if I get a letter saying that they want to hear me in a year's time, because that's encouraging, and at least they think I'm going to improve.
>
> Nic Dowton

- *Ask for the panel's Comment Sheets to find out what they thought of you.*

> Occasionally I phone up the office and ask them for comments on how I have played. The panel always write down their remarks and observations, so they've got something to which they can refer. If you do it this way, they can take time and come up with some good advice that might actually help you for your next audition. But if you phone up the principals themselves, that will put them on the spot and they may feel harassed. Creating such awkwardness might then jeopardize your chances of ever working with them, even if they were desperate. When I receive the Comment Sheet, I do take the advice they give on board. But I don't take it too seriously and completely change my playing because it is merely one panel's opinion.

The most frustrating thing that I find with the Comment Sheet, however, is when they haven't asked you to do anything differently in your audition. For instance, if they claim you were too quiet, it would just have taken a simple: 'Could you do that a bit louder please?', and you could have proved to them you could have done it. You have to be a mind-reader in this game, and a lot of the time you get it wrong. If you're going in for a second-flute audition, would they just want to see what sort of second-flute player you are, or would they want you to walk in with a big ego and play as if you are a principal? Who knows? Every panel is different, and there will be few times that you will get it right. But hopefully there will be some musicians listening to you who will see your potential.

Nic Dowton

Famous film stars don't always get the leading part in the latest movie. We too must get used to receiving the humbling:

Rejection Letter

This is part and parcel of our careers as musicians, and I know of players who have framed rejection letters and hung them on their wall. Once you have been rejected, try to understand why and gain enlightenment from your failure. Use it to your advantage. Were there any extracts you didn't know? What put you off? Did you play better than during your last audition? Did you feel relaxed at any point? Learn from your errors, and put a good spin on them. Otherwise it will merely have been a miserable experience.

If you play well in your audition but fail to get through the primary stages, then it may only be a matter of time before you succeed. Remember that music is subjective. Your playing style may not suit the 'Western Philharmonic' but be ideal for the 'Eastern Symphony'.

There is a fine line to be drawn between optimism and delusion, though. If you continue to fail, that should be a clear indication of a weakness that needs rectifying. The next chapter may help you to identify some of your faults. However, if you still have no joy, you may have to ask yourself the following question:

At What Point Should I Quit?

Exactly how many failed auditions you should endure before quitting is a serious question. It would be unwise to generalize. I have a colleague who applied for twenty-one auditions before jumping over that first hurdle and winning a trial. He obtained the position he wanted and soon after excelled himself, going on to better positions until he landed himself a plum job. Another successful musician who performed regularly in front of large audiences, paradoxically suffered from extreme audition nerves. It meant that he never achieved a single trial. But with determination, tenacity and serendipity he won the day. He is now a highly sought-after freelancer.

Many players would have come to other conclusions after so many failed attempts, and some would have decided to give up completely. If you feel you are in such a position, you know what to do. Ring up some major players, explain your predicament and book a series of lessons. Full-time players in top orchestras will have their ear close to the ground in matters of sound and style. Listen to their advice and follow the regime they prescribe. It is honesty that you need. And yet, if you have been out of college for a few years, you may have lost touch and find the truth difficult to accept. It can be difficult to establish, too. As in other 'walks of life,' in a misguided attempt to be kind, or sometimes out of cowardice, people are often evasive about the facts. I've many times heard someone say: 'Oh, well done, that really was most musical, I did enjoy that,' while at the same time writing a note to their orchestral fixer on the lines of: 'I never want to see this unmusical gibbon again.'

I will end the chapter with two more anecdotes. A distinguished colleague of mine, now retired, started off in my orchestra as second clarinet. For years, he regularly 'stepped up' to play principal; but when the principal job became vacant, he had to suffer the indignity of being auditioned. Unwillingly, he obliged. A few minutes into the audition, he flew into a terrible temper, kicked over the music-stand and stormed out of the room, cursing. Recounting this story to me, he laughed as he recalled the spectacle of vast numbers of sight-reading excerpts floating to the ground in slow motion. The conductor immediately ran out after him and found him in the lavatory. Convincing him that the audition had gone wonderfully, he coaxed him back into the audition room for a glass of wine. In those days, huge quantities of wine and bowls full of fruit would have covered the audition table. The alcohol and fruit were promptly consumed, the atmosphere improved and everyone became intoxicated. In his inebriated state, the conductor said: 'Right then, let's get on with the audition.' It was a serious request, and my friend was made to complete all the excerpts and set pieces. Needless to say, he no longer cared much, and he continued without further ado. He got the job and stayed in it for another twenty years, playing the most beautiful solo clarinet you have ever heard in your life.

My final anecdote comes from the panel. A principal flautist was holding an extra-work audition for his orchestra. He stopped the applicant mid-way through her prepared piece, and asked her to play a scale. This was a very unusual demand. But you should be prepared for anything. With a pregnant pause, she shook her head, put her flute down beside her body and silently walked towards the door. Just before turning the handle, with gritted teeth, she swung round and hissed: 'You ... bastard!' You see what we have to put up with on an audition panel.

You need to play well in auditions so that you can proceed to the next stage in your progress towards becoming an orchestral musician. Once you have been invited to play with a professional orchestra, you will be looked at from a new perspective. In the minds of ensemble players, the art of being able to play *with* others is far more important than being able to impress a panel. Your first professional rehearsal will put you to the test.

Chapter 5

Ensemble

'The greatest beauties of melody and harmony become faults
and imperfections when they are not in their proper place.'
Christoph Willibald Gluck, 1714–87

People either have the gift of awareness or not. Some youngsters come
in knowing the music, but then just crash on through without listening; and it is things like that which are really apparent.

Miriam Skinner

At music college no one prepared me for the profound aural
awareness that is required within an orchestra. I am talking about
the art of listening to other players so intently that you adapt to
them and become part of their playing; about possessing the
ability to get inside their vibrato and intonation; about blending
subtly into their instrumental colours, using identical articulation,
and matching phrasing and note-lengths.

I was taught to be a soloist. I was encouraged to be as virtuoso
as possible rather than concentrating on ensemble playing. I still
believe that this is probably the best way for individual instrumentalists to be taught. It is very thorough, and can lead to great
technical progress; but it seems that ensemble playing is usually
left to chance, and not taught. Perhaps this is because the heightened awareness you need to become a genuine ensemble player
comes from an inherent sensitivity that is impossible to achieve
solely through hard work and teaching.

It is not good enough merely to be able to play your own part. The
crucial thing is awareness of what is going on around you.

Jonathan Goodall

Real ensemble players have the ability to play in exact unison with
you, with a colour that blends together with your own to produce
a new sound. They dominate when needed, and then simply
vanish back into the texture. Intonation is not an issue for them

since they adjust and adapt imperceptibly (see the chapter on *Intonation*). Natural ensemble players are clairvoyant: they seem to know how and when you are about to play almost before you do. No words are needed; no excessive movement is required. They appear like magic alongside you.

> I've sat next to youngsters who basically have no knowledge of orchestral repertoire at all, and yet they eat it for breakfast because they have a sixth sense of where the music is going to go. They are aware of how the band is actually working, and unbeknown to themselves, they just don't put their foot in it. They know where to play; they know how to play; and they do it without thinking. They have an innate musical clock in them which enables them to play with what is going on. That is the jewel that I look for among orchestral players.
>
> Robert Chasey

Musicians who have played next to or near to talented and sensitive ensemble players will tell you how much joy it brings them, allowing them to scale new musical heights.

If you are not in this league, take heart, because:

- *As a young, inexperienced player, your ensemble qualities may not be fully developed and may need awakening.*

There are varying degrees of sensitivity in ensemble playing, and although true ensemble playing is a natural talent, like absolute pitch, I believe that students can improve enormously if they are pointed in the right direction.

> I never thought about such things as articulation and dynamics in any great depth until I started to work professionally. Before that, I just got caught up in playing the right notes – and then thinking: 'Great, I can play that.' You soon find out that there is so much more to it than that.
>
> Ben Hudson

How revealing it is when a new player is asked to blend a little better, or to listen to another player's note endings, and they look at you dumbfounded. By illustrating some of the ground-rules and fundamentals, I hope that many improvements will be possible for you. Encouraging your auditory senses to feed your mind will enable you to play in an ensemble with ease.

First, you must be aware that:

All Orchestras are Different

In a professional group of musicians, you will be dominated by the 'key' players who, with their years of experience within the ensemble, will have developed their own stamp of colour and blending, and of phrasing and vibrato. You should be able to hear such differences from the audience, but they will be even more apparent – and will be magnified tenfold – when you sit within an orchestra. They are not definitive or invariable as ideas in orchestras slowly develop and grow all the time, for many reasons. The addition of a new, innovative player, for example, can easily spark off a change in direction for their particular section; often it will have a knock-on effect that will motivate the whole orchestra. The principal conductor – and visiting maestros, too – will also bring in new ideas, with any luck inspiring the musicians on a daily basis. The musicians themselves will be constantly experimenting, and trying to make improvements. So you should look upon an orchestra as a live, organic being.

If you have just landed yourself with a full-time job, you will discover that there is plenty of time to get to know how to blend in with and fit into your orchestra's texture and style.

• *Your playing should gravitate naturally towards that of the orchestra.*

If you are exceptionally talented, you will find that their playing will be drawn towards yours as well. In either case this will happen gradually, without anyone really noticing.

As a newcomer to the freelance profession, though, you will have to be quick on your toes, and make sure that you do adapt to the orchestra you are playing with every day.

There are some orchestras that really go for it, with massive dynamic ranges; whilst others are more interested in the subtleties, so you have to control everything a little bit more, allowing the tone to come through. Some principals want their second player to play loudly so that they can bounce off the sound and feel more supported, whilst with others you've got to play right down because they don't want you to overshadow anybody else. Within the first two minutes, you must figure out what they want and then adapt accordingly.

Nic Dowton

Yesterday's orchestra may play at A = 441 Hz, use loads of vibrato and play on the loud side; whereas today's may be tuned at A = 440 Hz and be a much more sensitive group as far as their vibrato and dynamics are concerned. If you get things the wrong way round (and this is no exaggeration), you will never be asked back to that orchestra again, and, unlike in music college, you probably won't be told what you were doing wrong. Musicians can be very secretive: if you are doing the right thing, you will be asked back; if not, you won't. As a freelancer, you may ask whether you are fitting in satisfactorily and playing all right, but more than likely you will be told that everything is just fine, no matter what people are thinking. The only confirmation of your success will be whether you are re-booked.

> The best feeling of all is to be asked back into an orchestra with which you have just played. It means that they were happy with your playing, and that you did a good job. It is even better than getting the work in the first place.
>
> Emma Ringrose

If you are getting work through auditions but never being asked back, you are obviously at a high enough standard to work professionally but you must be doing something fundamentally wrong. Look through the rest of this chapter, as well as the *Surviving in the Orchestral Profession* chapter, and see whether you can identify your failings. If you can't fathom what the problem is, then, once again, you know what to do ... Ring a major player ... lesson ... advice!

When playing in an orchestra, you have to weigh up the ensemble jigsaw that confronts you, and then fit effortlessly into the correct position, as I have said. So the first thing is to:

Know Your Role

One of the crucial aspects of ensemble playing is to know whether at any particular time you are leading or following. The majority of students – as I have mentioned in the 'Orchestral Excerpts' section of the *Auditions* chapter, on page 64 – will only learn the important, solo lines at college, and yet the chances are against their taking such a position at the beginning of their career. Even if you do play a key role, you will not find yourself in the limelight all the time: you may be required to play with a more distinctive sound, and allowed to project yourself during your solo, but it may only be when the music requires it. As a solo orchestral player, you will have to discover how and when to metamorphose into a beautiful swan or a resplendent peacock, and, more importantly, to learn how then to become a chameleon so that you can blend immediately into the orchestral environment again.

Accompanying

Every ensemble player needs to be able to accompany. Even if you have just played the most important solo in the repertoire, you will need to let go of your ego and merge back into the ensemble, or perhaps cushion the subsequent soloist's sound, and permit the more important line to project. When you are playing such a supporting role, you must acquire 'musical radar' to allow the soloist the flexibility to use rubato. A true accompanist should be able to follow the lead line like glue without feeling sticky. When a really good accompanist is accompanying you, it is like wearing the most beautifully tailored clothes: they make you look good and feel light, and enable you to move as freely as you wish. Playing with a bad accompanist, on the other hand, is like carrying a donkey: it's heavy going, uncomfortable and a complete waste of time.

Whatever your role in the orchestra, you have to watch and listen like a hawk at all times and learn to blend.

Blending

Very little is taught about blending at music college: it seems not to be glamorous. Orchestral musicians must play with the collective's sound and style at the forefront of their minds. Learning the art of blending is therefore of paramount importance.

> The sound you have to make in an orchestra is one that will blend. Even as an experienced section player, it is something I still have to think about. Obviously you want to play at 100% and make a big sound; but if you project too much, you will stick out in the section. There are lots of ways of solving this. For example, if you are playing

high up on the E string in an exposed loud passage, you will need to use a faster bow speed and less pressure than you would if you were a soloist. It doesn't matter where you sit in the section: if you make a sound that is very individual, even if it's full of character, it won't work if it does not blend.

On my trial, all I had done up to that point was to play with my college symphony orchestra, and it was never really an issue there. There is the old joke about the first violin section of a college symphony orchestra consisting of sixteen soloists all playing the same thing; and there was an element of that. Nobody really wants to subjugate themselves into blending in with the rest of the section, or becoming unified. You're there to show off.

So when I came into a professional orchestra, it was completely different. I had to find out how to fit in, and I had to find out pretty quickly. I started off in the second violins, and the principal told me straight away: 'You are making a big sound there: that's great for a Brahms sonata but you shouldn't use such a wide vibrato, and try to use more of a veiled sound.' He told me that early on, and I took his advice. He didn't need to, and I could have been offended that he was criticizing my playing; but I think it is important to listen to such advice. You don't have to take it, as you make your own decisions.

I've learnt since that you need a much wider variety of sounds – from small to enormous – but the point is: it has to be the right one for the situation. It's a secret in section-playing that you do need to learn.

Julian Gregory

In order to blend in, you may have to create a more dilute sound than you would wish to produce in a solo recital; and if you find a more dilute sound enhances the colour whilst a soloistic one distorts it, you will know which one you should use. I demonstrate this in class by getting two players to play a unison note. I ask one to be the more dominant player and the other to be the blender. Once the dominant player has started playing, the blender should be able to enter without being heard. There is usually a conflict at first, with excessive vibrato, the distortion of sounds and clashes of intonation; but after much experimentation the tone can become as one. With effort, the colour should blossom and result in a greater beauty than would be achieved otherwise. When we all agree that the blending has been successful, I then ask the less dominant player to play their note to the class in exactly the way that fused the two instruments together. This often surprises students as the veiled and dilute colour that is required to weave the sounds together is not one that they would have ever considered worth achieving. As the student progresses, they will acquire a palette of blending colours that are not so 'hazy' and will be equal in beauty to any solo sound. These sounds will have many of their harmonics suppressed (see the harmonic-spectrum frequency graphs on pages 159–66).

Combining this ability to blend with all the other skills listed in this chapter, you will become an orchestral player of note – although there is an area, vital to blending, that isn't discussed here in detail. Intonation is such an enormous subject that it requires and deserves a chapter of its own. It is near the end of the book. However, please note that if you can't play in tune with the rest of your ensemble, it will be impossible for you to blend with them no matter how hard you try.

Vibrato

If you ask any section leader, and especially woodwind principals, to list the commonest problems with extras and deputies being able to blend, then vibrato will invariably come close to the top. Some of them will say that most players who come in have 'too much,' while others will say they have 'too little'. There is also the 'too wide' and 'too shallow' kind of wobble. Perhaps the real problem is that vibrato is a personal flavour that is dictated by taste.

… in Nature

In 1960, a scientist named Dr Fritz Winckel wrote in his book *Music, Sound and Sensation* that there is a natural vibrato that is found throughout the animal kingdom, and that all animals use and respond to some sort of fluctuation within their songs and calls. It is interesting to note that animals pay no attention to artificial sounds that are produced by electronic equipment (without a wobble) until a vibrato is added. Humans, too, find it difficult to ignore sounds that have a fluctuation, but we can quite easily sleep through an electric hum, the whirr of a fan and the sound of a regularly ticking clock – and only wake up when the sound stops.

... in Music

Vibrato is a fluctuation in pitch that is used by some instrumentalists to colour their tone, and that allows them to intensify the passion and expression in a phrase. The techniques for accomplishing this vary according to each instrument. Nevertheless, there are two basic rules that apply to *all* instruments, and that are frequently broken. First, you should imagine the pitch you are playing as a single line, and the pitch variation that results from the vibrato as an oscillating sine wave. This wave should be evenly positioned on either side of the fundamental pitch line. Favouring one side rather than the other will cause intonation problems, and if you make the pitch variation extreme, it will add a bilious flavour to your sound.

The second rule is that you should imagine your tone as a set of tram lines, the vibrato wave being placed in between them. As the emotion of the music changes, you can and should change the speed and intensity of your vibrato, and even eliminate it altogether if the music dictates. But at no point should the vibrato wave be outside the tram lines: vibrato should always remain within, and therefore be shallower than, the tone.

Obviously, in a professional symphony orchestra you cannot always play with the type of vibrato you would use in a solo concert. And so, as I have said in relation to ensemble, you must use your ears.

- *Listen to the players around you, and hear the speed and intensity of vibrato they are using.*

Using a speed that is much faster, slower, wider or shallower than that of the people with whom you are playing will cause the colours to clash: you will stick out and the sounds will not blend. If you are accompanying the most beautiful solo performed by a musician with a scintillatingly gorgeous vibrato and your wobble, for instance, is slow and wide like that of a car starting on a cold morning, you will probably never set foot in that organization again. As much thought should be dedicated to vibrato as to sound in general. They are closely interconnected, the vibrato being the life within the timbre and not an addition placed haphazardly on top of it.

- *Practice vibrato with an array of contrasting speeds and intensities.*

Personally, I try to use a vibrato that is close to, but has no exact correlation to, the speed of the music. This way, you can be sure that the strong emphasis of the vibrato never aligns with a major beat of the bar. But keep this in mind:

• *You should always use a colour of sound and a depth of vibrato that will marry well and will be relevant to the music.*

Care must also be taken not to use a vibrato that can be misinterpreted as an articulation from a distance.

Note-Endings

It is a delicious experience when the ninety musicians of a symphony orchestra finish a phrase together with a beautifully polished note-ending that dissolves into silence in the same way that the sea sometimes dissolves into the sky. When those same ninety people play 'hell for leather' at breakneck speed, and then without any warning stop dead in their tracks, blatantly defying all Newton's laws of gravity, then you know that you are listening to a very tight ensemble indeed. However, if just one of those players doesn't taper their sound at exactly the same speed as everyone else, to create that polished note-ending, or if one player polishes too much when everyone else stops dead, you will have lost everything and destroyed the perfect ensemble. It only takes one person to pull that loose thread in a perfect garment to ruin it, and if that one player is you, it may be time for you to move out of the area.

The ending of a note is like a tail. Sometimes it is long and decays over several seconds like a bell. Sometimes it is short and delicate like the sound of a glockenspiel; and it can be brutally abrupt as in the artificial finality of dampened timpani. With note-endings, I always try to picture the sound visually. Depending on the musical context, I may imagine it as the arc of a projectile falling from a cliff – or perhaps being thrown into the air and then plummeting down again. I can then visualize placing my taper on top of everyone else's. If mine has a different curve from the others, then I'm wrong. A note-ending should be an exact fit, in the same way that many transparencies of the same picture placed on top of one another should look as one.

• *Experiment with the speed of taper at the end of notes.*

By imitating the natural decay of other instruments' note-endings, while you are becoming attuned and sensitive to the whole issue, you will soon find that your ensemble feels less ragged. For a time, this may result in your playing slightly shorter endings than those of the surrounding instruments; and, whilst this may be wrong, it is preferable, for at least you won't be heard in any of the musical gaps, and it may buy you time while you learn to re-calibrate your note 'end-o-meter.'

While experimenting with the taper, you might also like to try relaxing the sound a little (after the initial attack) when playing non-melodic, accompanying notes. This will add a lighter quality to your tone as well as making blending much easier. You won't have to do this all the time, but you may like the effect. By playing a fraction more lightly and tapering the notes in this way, you may discover that you can hear the blend a little better. If the phrases within the ensemble suddenly become clearer and cleaner than before, obviously *you* have been holding onto *your* notes longer than everybody else and muddying the water. Try it out – you may have been annoying the players around you.

It is worth pointing out that, in theory, it is possible to play staccatos on wind instruments that are shorter and more truncated than any pizzicatos that can be played on stringed instruments. To continue on this theme, violin pizzicatos are naturally shorter than pizzicatos on a 'cello (unless they are dampened). Wind instruments have small reverberation chambers compared to their stringed cousins, and so they may find themselves needing to elongate their notes slightly in order to blend. Adding such an ultra-quick note-ending, or tail, to wind and even to brass staccatos when they are combined with a pizzicato string section, a harp or a percussive instrument, will result in more 'bell-like' sounds rather than merely short and abrupt ones. The notes will fit better into the timbre. But with *all* note-endings – providing the music requires uniformity – make sure that you decay at the same rate. Otherwise the effect will be lost.

Articulation

Whereas note-ending is concerned with the important matter of how each note should finish, articulation deals with the note's beginning. If you can sort both these things out, all you will have to worry about is what to do with the sound in the middle. Only kidding! There's much more to it than that.

For me, articulation is the tool with which I weave the written note into the musical texture in the way that a painter uses a brush to stroke paint onto his canvas. An artist would never only have one paintbrush; and yet we come across musicians who only have a couple of ways of articulating. Artists will have various sizes of brush, all of them with different textures of bristle. They will have an assortment of pastels, crayons and pencils. Musicians, too, need as many articulations as possible – including one that has no attack and can appear from nowhere – to give us the flexibility to paint an inspirational picture with our music. In the *Conductors* chapter, there is an exercise that helps you to pinpoint and develop the beginnings of your notes. It will take a lot of experimenting for you to find the wide array of articulation 'tools' that are available. I indicated in the previous chapter that my articulation while playing with a clarinet might have to be longer and less bouncy than when I played with pizzicato strings. It might also have to be on the smooth side when tonguing with a horn, and more brittle when playing with staccato oboes.

There is a fine art to playing in an ensemble. For example, a good second player will vary their attack whilst playing in unison so that they support but, at the same time, do not interfere with the line. You learn the art by doing a lot of it and listening. You also have to get to know the person sitting next to you personally. That is when an orchestra becomes an orchestra and not just ninety individuals.

Patrick Addinall

- *Practise a variety of articulations: imagine each time that you are playing with a different instrument; and see if you can hear any difference between your results.*

Each instrument has its own natural characteristics and its range of dynamics; and within each symphony orchestra there will be players who have managed to expand their articulation techniques as well as their tonal capabilities. It is obvious. You have to listen, to be alert and to use your developing senses in order to fit precisely within another instrument's sound or attack.

Rhythm

'Rhythm is order, not the order that moves with cosmic precision
but that of humanity with all its mercurial emotions.
Within us is a flexible human metronome – the heart.'
Joseph Hofmann, 1876–1957,
American pianist born in Poland.
(He was equally gifted in music, mathematics, science and mechanics.)

My teacher once played our flute class a recording of the legendary countertenor Alfred Deller. The excerpt he played was a song
with a dotted rhythm throughout. What fascinated us was the
freedom and variation he got from this simple mathematical
calculation. A pedant would insist that each group of notes should
be executed in an exactly identical way, yet in this example no two
groups were the same. When he sang, it sounded totally natural
as he maintained a lilting, flexible pulse; and – the clever part –
the listener would not have known about this freedom without
analysing his rhythm. If, instead, the song had been sung metro-
nomically, we would have found the interpretation unacceptably
boring by comparison. This was the point of the exercise.

For a month during my first summer holiday when I was at
college, I studied the later recordings of Artur Rubinstein: the
Chopin *Nocturnes* and Schumann's *Fantasiestücke, op.12*, were
particular favourites. I followed the scores, conducted his rubato
and tried to analyse the magic he attained (see the 'Learn to Conduct' section in the *Performing Philosophies* chapter, on page 46).
The knowledge I gathered then has been a major influence in my
music-making to this day. But first things first:

• *Check your basic sub-division.*

Here is a simple exercise but a valuable one. Get a pulse going on
a metronome and start sub-dividing the beat by tapping the table
in front of you with a pencil. First, drum out 2 to a pulse, and
go on from there. Trying 3, 4, 5, 6, 7 and 8 as well should be
sufficient. Make sure that the 5s and 7s are equal sub-divisions
rather than being grouped into easier, unequal clusters. If you
wish, you can extend this exercise by incorporating first basic and
then more complex rhythmical patterns, thus improving your
sight-reading ability. An additional and useful variation would be
to practise syncopations. Many students find playing continuous

'off-beats' difficult to achieve without rushing, slowing down or sounding tense. You might set the metronome to a faster pulse and then try to tap out evenly spaced syncopated notes, coaxing them to sound relaxed without any hint of catching up or slowing down to the beat. Playing musically with a metronome is an important discipline. So if you find any of these tasks difficult, repeat them until they become natural. Eventually you should be able to do them all without any tension. External jerky movements and foot-tapping can be offputting to other people and should not be necessary, since a natural rhythm should exist deep within you. If, however, you continually falter and make little progress with these exercises, you should see a specialist who will analyse your rhythmical deficiency. If you find yourself in this situation, you really shouldn't proceed with the rest of the section here because attempting a natural rubato will more than likely generate bad rhythm in your playing. Once these experiments have been achieved with ease, you can go beyond the understanding of mathematical rhythm and reach a new freedom.

Rubato

Rubato comes from the Italian word meaning 'to rob', although in music there is no victim as the stolen time is usually given back immediately. If you think of music as a strip of elastic, you would be able to draw musical sub-divisions on it and watch the spacing change as you pulled on either side. You would be able to stretch it this way and that, and it would still fall back into shape afterwards. If you stretched it too much and too often, you would lose the elasticity and, with it, the shape of your performance. Visualizing the relationship between rhythms in this way is helpful as many players fail to observe the natural spacing that occurs as music is stretched and contracted. There are a few exceptions to this 'expansion' rule, the most famous being that of Mahler's Fifth Symphony where he clearly writes that the triplet figure (marked 'flying') should always be played with an accelerando.

Mahler, Symphony No. 5, 1st movement, bars 8–13

This produces a temporary freedom and a tug of emotions that momentarily leaves the surrounding tempi behind, and adds to the exhilarating atmosphere. In this symphony – and others, too – Mahler has passed down to us a playing tradition that breaks this rule even further. Often, he asks for rhythmical figures (particularly dotted rhythms) to sound the same throughout a work, irrespective of tempo changes or rubato. In slow sections, for example, this may result in dotted rhythms being performed close to the lengths of double-dotted ones, with a longer first note and a quicker ending. Without such knowledge, though, someone following the score might be confused as to why the printed rhythms are so different from those in a performance.

Of course there is some music that requires continuous rhythmic – and rigid – precision. For example, in the first movement of Shostakovich's Seventh Symphony, there is a long section with side-drum (a sinister *bolero*) depicting the relentless marching of German troops towards Leningrad during the Second World War. At first they are far away. The drum-beat gradually builds up as they lay siege to the city. One iota of metronomic deviation will ruin the effect of the entire passage:

Shostakovich, Symphony No. 7, 1st movement

Just before this section, there is a passage of tranquillity and peace. It depicts the people's hopes and expectations in August 1941, a month before the Germans arrive, and the peaceful and joyous life of the workers, thinkers and creators who were all to become warriors. This section by contrast requires an organically moving and flowing pulse. Sometimes with a pendulum motion:

Shostakovich, Symphony No. 7, 1st movement

And at other times with a poise and a flexible rhythm that should always sound totally natural:

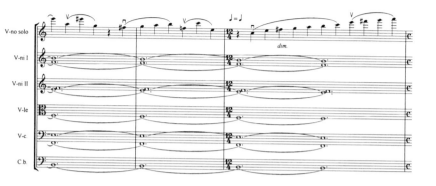

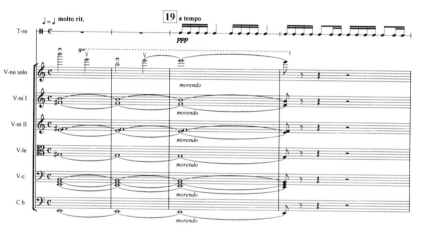

(The above extracts are from
Symphony No. 7, *Leningrad*, by Shostakovich.
© Copyright Boosey & Hawkes Music Publishers Ltd
Reproduced by permission of Boosey & Hawkes Music Publishers Ltd)

If an orchestra were to play these sections without an intelligent freedom of pulse, they would sound heartless. Once you are fortunate enough to have experienced this kind of musical liberation, anything less expressive will seem callous by comparison. Top orchestras with excellent conductors can achieve such a level of innate rhythm. But under a conductor with few leadership skills (see the *Conductors* chapter), maintaining rhythm can be like practising synchronized calligraphy on a double-decker bus. As I have said before, you must latch onto what is going on around you, listen and fit in.

- *Even if you believe that the rhythm you are playing is correct and that other people are wrong, don't pick a fight as no one will win, and the resulting sound will be messy.*
- *Once you are all playing as a unit, you can discuss the rhythm of certain passages.*

As a solo player, you may be playing the offending rhythm yourself. Then perhaps, in a rehearsal, you could subtly show everyone how you felt the passage should really go. If others listen and agree, they may adopt your version. If they don't, and the conductor fails to rectify the problem, forget about it since the most important rhythmical ensemble skill is to be able to:

- *Play as one, for rhythmical discrepancies are 'poison' to ensemble players.*

There is a passage at the beginning of Stravinsky's ballet *Petrushka* that few orchestras play accurately:

Using your newly acquired conducting technique (see page 46), try singing the top line of this extract while beating crotchets. Watch out for the bars containing 7s where *only* the first note (or rest) aligns with any beat. Take care placing the 'sixth' of the seven quavers – especially at figure four (the last G). Many place this note before, or on, the last beat of that bar. Mathematically it should come immediately afterwards. Other common errors with this short passage include playing the triplet figure as a mordent in addition to rushing, or playing irregular 5s, 7s and 8s. I teach my students to play this passage in every possible way so that, whatever bands they play with, they can always fit in. If you feel strongly about how certain rhythms should go and cannot agree to compromise in such matters, or indeed in relation to any musical ideals, perhaps you should become a conductor. Otherwise ...

- 'Go *with the flow*.'

Dynamics

or how loudly do you want me to play?

> It is difficult to understand the extremes of dynamics that are needed when playing in a symphony orchestra. You may believe that you are playing really softly or very loudly, but in fact that will be nowhere near what is required.
>
> Ben Hudson

It is indeed hard to work out how loudly you should play in an orchestra. As we find in life, when the ambient dynamics increase around us, we speak louder to compensate. You may have been in the situation when you are talking to people in a crowded room and suddenly everyone becomes silent. You can then be embarrassed by how loudly you seemed to be talking – or shouting. You were in fact only competing with the surrounding noise to try and hear yourself. Similarly, in an orchestra it is easy to force your sound. It takes great discipline and experience to avoid this because when you first play in an orchestra, everything sounds loud and confusing. But:

- *As the brain relaxes, the ear can be trained.*

In time, your hearing will become so acute that you will be able to pick out the viola line or the third desk of 'cellos, even when the trumpets are playing fortissimo.

To begin with:
• *Listen to the people closest to you.*
The contract players in the orchestra will probably know how loudly their principal will want them to play at any particular moment, and so you should copy them. What we all want is a glorious bloom to the sound from a distance. If you play too loudly you can easily ruin this, and, if you do, I'm sure you will be reported to the section-leader.

You should note that volume is not just produced by everyone playing at their maximum dynamics as the quality would then be lost. In acoustics we are taught that two players do not produce twice the volume of sound. With 'masking' – the erasure of one sound by another – we actually need about ten people playing at the same dynamics level to produce the perception that the loudness has doubled. You must therefore always think of tone production in conjunction with dynamics, along with the number of musicians playing your line.

For wind and brass players, volume is a more difficult subject as quite often an 'under part' may suddenly have a solo: it may be your first professional date playing third or fourth flute in Mahler's Seventh Symphony; and there are moments when you will have to play a line that is more important than the principal's. You will have to emerge, sing your phrase beautifully, and then disappear.

ppp-fff

The human ear can tolerate up to 120 decibels (db) before experiencing pain. According to David Butler in his book *The Musician's Guide to Perception and Cognition* that level is a *trillion* times louder than a sound at the threshold of hearing. And yet we only have eight basic dynamic markings, from *ppp* to *fff*. I conclude from this that dynamics in music are and will remain flexible, personal and relative.

The ear interprets sound through a series of hair cells on the cochlea that vibrate backwards and forwards in the inner ear. We are born with around 30,000 of these hair cells, and if they vibrate a lot, the sound is loud, and if they barely shake, the sound is quiet. After a loud concert you may hear ringing in your ears, or even experience a certain dullness for a few hours – or, in extreme cases, a few days. This is because the hairs will have vibrated so vigorously that they will have been bent. In such a case, they won't respond in the usual way, and will need time to recover fully before once again standing proud to work normally. Once you reach 140db, the hair cells can start to break, after which they cannot be repaired naturally. It is interesting to note that a cymbal can peak at 146db, although the European directive advises ear-protection to be worn above 90db. It is proposed that this limit should be lowered to 85db in 2005.

Back-Desk Soloists

How many times have you heard a choir ruined by one loud voice which jars against the rest of the ensemble? This can happen whether the singer concerned is good or bad. Playing too loudly, proving your worth, is a mistake that many new freelancers make when playing in an orchestra for the first time. They intentionally play *forte* throughout the rehearsal to let everyone hear 'how good they are', and then practise their concertos in the orchestral breaks. I remember being told off myself by the lead viola player while warming up at my first professional gig. He shouted: 'No concertos in the band room!' Later, while I was practising my part for that evening's concert, the same violist growled: 'No prizes for finishing before the rest of us.' If this is an extreme case, which could have upset a more sensitive novice, such encounters can be very annoying even to hardened professionals. Playing louder than other people may wreck a rehearsal, and unless you are on the point of playing a concerto, you shouldn't be showing off during the tea break, either. You should be buying the teas.

It is worth mentioning that there are many contract players who could play as soloists if they wished. I remember once waking up in a hotel room and hearing a most beautiful solo violin playing part of a Mozart concerto. It was confusing to me, as the sound was considerably better than that of the soloist with whom we were touring. Intrigued, I skulked around the hallways to find where it had come from. It was an education to me when a back-desk player eventually left the room from which that heavenly, intoxicating sound had issued. Such players don't show off in orchestral rehearsals because it's not their job to do so.

Finally

Everyone makes ensemble mistakes. The art is to learn from them and to try not to make the same ones again. As I have said:

- *If you do make an error but rectify it straight away, that could actually work in your favour as an inexperienced yet talented player.*
- *Musicians can sometimes be very charitable as long as you are willing to learn and accept that you are doing something wrong. They are intolerant towards those who haven't a clue.*

We're very sympathetic to young players coming in. We know that it's hard at first, so while we help occasionally, we don't constantly point out problems. The sort of players that are going to fit in easily, tend to be perceptive about what is going on. If you have to tell them everything, then it's not going to work. If they've got the qualities that I'm looking for – good sound, rhythm, intonation and an awareness of what is going on – then it doesn't matter if they make mistakes at the beginning because you know they'll come through in the end.

Jonathan Goodall

Chapter 6

Nerves

'We must have music to drive our fears away.'
Noël Coward, playwright, 1899–1973,
(© The estate of Noël Coward)

Achieving confidence is a constant battle. But you have to expect that if you are going to be a performer. If you've done the work, got the technique and have a reasonable temperament, then you should be able to get through the difficult patches. Although, however much you prepare away from the orchestra, it is very different when you are actually sitting there. I always think the pressure is like snooker or golf – that final putt on the eighteenth green, with cameras and a crowd watching you. Relaxed concentration is the key.

Jonathan Goodall

At worst, the worries of performing can lead to you sweating, to uncontrollable shakes and panic attacks and to you even feeling sick. But nerves can also help you to excel. The increased flow of adrenalin can move you into a higher gear and create extra excitement and atmosphere.

We all suffer from nerves; some of us more than others. I have known players who have had successful performing careers but have still suffered terribly from nerves. One of them, a soloist as well as an orchestral musician, used to get so anxious before going on stage, that he was in fact often sick. There are also musicians who, after years of not feeling anything, have suddenly lost their nerve and haven't been able to continue to perform. On occasion, I have played next to people who have shaken so much that I have become nervous myself, wondering whether or not they were going to be able to play. I have performed concertos live on broadcasts world-wide without so much as a heart-flutter or a shaky knee, and then been surprised at how nervous I was the next day while playing a relatively easy orchestral concert in front of a few hundred people.

'We say of a bridge that it is under *stress* (from the constant traffic flow, for instance, or from the action of the elements) and that it, the bridge, *strains*. The bridge suffers wear and tear and may crack or collapse as a result – not of stress, but of strain. Stress is a stimulus, strain a response. Clearly it is the response that causes a problem, not the stimulus; after all, many bridges have withstood centuries of unremitting stress. The stress of life is permanent and inevitable, and in itself it is neither negative nor undesirable. Witness the many healthy musicians who thrive under the most stressful situations, including baring their souls in front of hundreds or thousands of people.'

Pedro de Alcantara,
*Indirect Procedures: A Musician's Guide
to the Alexander Technique,* 1997
(Reproduced by permission of Oxford University Press)

We should also be aware of how dull the musical world would probably be without there being any kind of nerves at all, especially those nerves that can create an atmosphere where you sense that two thousand hearts are beating together in anticipation. Without them, live performances would lose their appeal.

We must now ask:

Why Do You Get Nervous?

Are your nerves a reflex reaction to the tensions of performing, or perhaps due to some fundamental insecurity you may have about your playing? You will have to diagnose which type you are vulnerable to so that you can work out what course of action you should take. We all sometimes feel that we can't play as well as we might. But why is this? When we are young, it is common for us not to feel any nerves at all, certainly not to the same extent as we do when we mature. Can we conclude that nerves evolve as we develop our techniques? One explanation may be that when we are young, we are more carefree, and everything seems easy, and fun, too. I also believe that difficulties do intensify as their importance increases. You may have had the experience of playing through a work that seems easy a week before a gig, but finding it impossibly difficult on the big day. The same piece may well become easier again after the concert. Does this mean that to play well you should stop caring? Of course not. However, some of my best performances have been when I have been so relaxed that I have been able to detach myself from the technical problems of my instrument and have just played. To be capable of doing this, you must have reached a certain level of musicality, as well as being completely fluent on your instrument.

As you progress, you will become aware of how you ought to be able to play. You will understand what is possible, and appreciate how difficult playing your instrument really is. A flute professor once told a colleague of mine: 'Don't practise too much; it'll only make it worse.' While I totally disagree with this statement, it is true that, as you improve, your ears become more discerning and you uncover new faults. You may feel that you are in fact getting worse. And yes. Occasionally you may have to take a couple of steps backwards in order to correct fundamental flaws. Such a backward movement will only be temporary so long as you continue to practise.

• *Practice is cumulative. There is no substitute.*

I remember visiting my parents after my first term at music college and finding that they were surprised I was still working on the same exercises and studies as before. They expected me to have moved on. I also remember a friend of my father's asking me: 'Have you finished learning the flute yet?' as if it was something one completes like a thesis, or a shopping list. Parents who are reading this please note: no one ever finishes learning their instrument. Whether you are a beginner, a music student or a master, there is always room for improvement. Playing a musical instrument is like caring for a prize-winning garden. It takes years to cultivate and build up and a lifetime to maintain. You cannot leave it to look after itself. Abandoning it for just a few days will give you extra work in the coming weeks. Your playing will be continually pulling in the opposite direction to where you want to go. (See 'Keeping in Shape' and 'Holidays' in the *Surviving in the Orchestral Profession* chapter, on pages 214 and 216.) Twenty-five years on, I'm still doing similar practice exercises.

Practice

• *It does not make you perfect but it will help you get close.*

If the stress you are under is because you feel that you can't play a particular passage well enough, then perhaps practice is the key. Under duress, your flaws could include an unstable sound quality as you diminuendo, or perhaps the inability to play a passage sufficiently fast.

By scrutinizing your methods, you will increase the efficiency of your practice.

• *Through hard, intelligent work you will gain confidence and come to believe that you can play a passage perfectly.*

Such new confidence may enable you to conquer your nerves. It will not be the reward for a few minutes' extra work but the pay-off from real practice.

For example:

• *Try learning all the technically difficult passages by heart.*

This intensifies the learning process. For practical reasons, and also through laziness, we often learn pieces superficially without spending the time to delve deep into the music. By slowing down the rate of learning, i.e. by practising sections from memory, we will have to work longer – visualizing the notes in order to etch in their patterns. The additional time spent working in this manner will give us the opportunity to understand the harmonies and structure of a work so that we can begin to interpret it. Profound practice of this kind has many benefits. It not only enables us to appreciate the music better. In the stress of a concert, the notes will play themselves.

> 'You should have the score in your head,
> not your head in the score.'
> Hans von Bülow,
> pianist and conductor, 1830–94

Nerve Targets

With experience, you will discover where your nerves are focused. The areas concerned will differ from player to player, but once you identify them, you will be able to redouble your practising of particular passages (or techniques) and attempt to mitigate the effects. If your difficulty is lip-tremor or bow-shake, then try holding the offending notes for twice or even four times as long each time you practise. If diminuendos are the problem, practise to the extremes of the dynamic range.

- *Continually pushing out your boundaries will enable your potential to be fully realized.*

If you are constantly extending your playing into new and higher realms, your performing standards will also be raised, even when you are under pressure.

- *Disciplined practice and patience are usually all that is required to combat minor nerves.*

Split It Up

- *It is wise to spread your practice out over a reasonable period of time.*

I advise my students to come back repeatedly to their studies throughout the day. My belief is: one can learn, improve and achieve more by doing three groups of 45 minutes of practice, for example, than playing for 135 minutes without a break. I'm sure you've been in the situation, while doing a long stretch of practice, where your mind seizes up as well as your fingers, arms, shoulders and back. Once you start going round in circles, you are practising mindlessly: you won't be learning anything useful, and you could be doing serious damage.

- *Don't get obsessed.*

Repeating one passage over and over again without applying your mind can lead to inflexible, non-spontaneous playing. Tension may follow and, at worst, lead to tendonitis and repetitive strain injury. For the most effective practice, and for achieving the fastest results:

- *Make sure your mind is always 'in gear' when you are working, and have regular, reasonable-sized practice-sessions when you continually insert 'that bit' you find so difficult.*

I encourage the use of several music stands to accomplish this. Students will have their 'dilemmas' close at hand instead of having to search through a stockpile of music, and wasting valuable time.

Students should perhaps complete their last practice session as late as possible in the day and begin their first as early as is sociably acceptable. For me, having the shortest possible gap between these two sessions keeps the muscles I require for playing strong and supple, and helps me to maintain my form.

- *It is not just the amount of work you do but also the frequency of your sessions that will aid your progress.*

It is incredible to what a degree the brain will continue to learn passages and study finger-patterns in between your practice sessions. Even when you merely look at a section of music and don't play it at all, your brain will be learning.

Visualization

For years, I have been advocating the rehearsing of complex patterns, difficult leaps and legato phrases in one's mind. Science now shows that this method does in fact allow the brain to study and absorb. While you are imagining that you are playing, your brain creates synaptic pathways through your brain cells as if you were actually practising. That is not the most remarkable fact. Studies at the University of Iowa show that when you are using such a visualization technique, the brain also sends electrical signals to the muscles involved and can strengthen them significantly.

The above information was taken from the BBC's *The Human Mind,* presented and written by Professor Robert Winston. However, these facts should be treated cautiously and they are not intended to encourage virtual practice instead of the real thing.

- *There is nothing like real practice to set you free and become totally flexible, to allow you to explore your musicality and watch your nerves dissolve.*

When you are absolutely fluent on your instrument, nothing should get in the way. This is how I was taught, and it usually works. You aim to be in total control so that you can enter the texture of the music and simply float away. When this happens, you will enjoy the music, and the performance will seem to be over too soon. I have been 'inside' the fabric of the composer's score and become completely absorbed by the colours of the orchestral painting on several occasions in my career. I was able to hear my flute playing itself, detached from the techniques of blowing and fingering. In total control, by thought alone. I can best explain it as an 'out of instrument experience'. As I indicated in the first chapter, though, moments like these don't occur often. When they do, you become addicted, and crave for more.

Don't Worry ...

Worrying is a major problem for musicians. It is possible to worry all day long about the problems and stresses of orchestral life. Worrying about worrying makes things worse. And so you need to find a way of coping.

• *Learn to put all your problems away when you pack up your instrument.*

You must be disciplined and learn not to worry about concerts, difficult phrases, articulated passages, etc, after your practice is finished. You must hand your problems over to your 'worry doll'. Guatemalan children have worry dolls to which they tell all their worries before going to sleep at night. The belief is that, overnight, the dolls will ponder over their troubles while they sleep soundly. If you continue to be concerned about something, get your instrument out and work a little longer; or look at the score, or listen to a recording. Don't allow your worries to fester. As I have said, your problems may sort themselves out between your practice sessions, and it does not help anybody if you worry twenty-four hours a day. You will become ill and it will be distressing for your family and friends. The idea of putting all your problems away together with your instrument was passed on to me by an oboist who sat next to me for eight years. I remember asking him whether he was worried about a specific passage, at which point he introduced me to his philosophy. He did, however, carry this idea to an extreme once when, on a German tour, a spring on his oboe broke moments before a performance. Dexterously, he fiddled around with a rubber-band and improvised a mechanism that would get him through the concert. After the performance, he told me that he had the equipment to attach a new spring. But as soon as he put his oboe away, he promptly forgot all about it. I'll never forget his flabbergasted expression as he opened the case at the next rehearsal, affronted that the oboe hadn't repaired itself!

The Public

The commonest fear causing nerves is to do with that terrifying beast – the public. You know they will be listening to you, watching you and paying good money to hear you. So you had better play well. The public will always be there listening unless you are another Glen Gould. He always preferred recording studios to the concert hall and adopted this form of music-making exclusively towards the end of his life. There is an interesting point to be made here. If successful, I believe we can go 'full circle' in our performance journey.

The Performing Circle

As beginners, we look inwards, trying to improve while attempting to play the correct notes. The next stage involves us in playing for relations at Christmas. Maybe it is here that our nerves are born. We are now entertainers and possibly becoming a little self-conscious. When we reach the third stage, we are pretty advanced, but our nerves may have multiplied. We will have to learn to combat them here if we are to attempt a performing career. At the fourth stage, we will have found a way of either coping with our nerves or else suppressing them as we will have become experienced artistes, performing numerous concerts, and impressing thousands of people, critics and managers.

There is a final stage, which Glen Gould attained when he moved on from impressing to reaching for the love of art and capturing the ethereal. You are playing for yourself on each occasion, and riding towards your zenith. If the audience has little understanding of the music and applauds between movements, it is of no importance. If you are playing to an empty concert hall, it makes no difference to you, as you are playing in the completed circle, joining the composer and exploring the music together with him.

> 'I'm addicted to music not audiences.'
> Miles Davis, jazz-trumpeter, 1926–91
> (© 2004 Miles Davis Properties, LLC.
> Reproduced by permission/All rights reserved)

There are artists of many kinds who create art with no thought of selling it. They create for art's sake and I know of wonderful musicians who do not perform. But this should not make them any less musicians. Perhaps, in the realms of true artistry, it ought to make them more so. However, since this book deals with orchestral playing in a commercial world, let's get back to reality.

In relation to the audience, we are basically entertainers and we have to earn a living.

I remember one of the first orchestral meetings I attended as a contract player. In essence, my orchestra had been a recording orchestra, performing twice a week to an empty studio, and with the occasional public concert thrown in for good measure. At that meeting, there was to be a vote on a new direction it could take. It was being proposed that we should become much more of a commercial and concert-giving orchestra than we had ever been in our fifty years' history. I was amazed at a 'cellist's comment objecting to the new proposal: 'I didn't join this orchestra to play music in concerts for other people to listen to.' He was serious!

• *Getting used to playing to an audience usually just takes time.* Some musicians are natural performers, adoring and desiring the public's attention, while a few are so laid back they can't seem to 'get their act together' until an audience is present. Occasionally, on the other hand, one finds performers who put up imaginary shields between themselves and the audience, and only just tolerate the fact that there have to be members of the public listening or the orchestra wouldn't exist. There are also a small minority who never really adapt to the audience's presence at all. Speaking for myself, I never quite know how I am going to feel with the audience until I start playing. At the beginning of my career, I tried to ignore the audience completely, but I have gradually learned to:

• *Enjoy communicating with them through the music.*
Communicating and playing the music for the composer usually helps me to get over my concert jitters. We must remember that the audience is there to have a good time. They are not there to be ignored, and they are not there to find faults in your playing, either. So you must continually remind yourself:

• *The public are at your concert to enjoy themselves, to lose themselves in an artistic experience.*

'Music ... it takes me to the other side.'
L.S. Lowry, painter 1887–1976

The audience want to be entertained, educated and emotionally transported, as I say. If they feel that you are nervous, they will be nervous too and possibly enjoy the concert less.

The pressures in a recording session are unlike those in a concert. When a concert begins, the music is set in motion and nothing will stop the performance. You know that you can only make one attempt to get it right. In a recording, the stresses are different.

Red-Light Nerves

At the beginning of my career, my staple musical diet consisted of recording two or three times a week in a soulless studio with nothing to inspire me barring the steel microphones, the standard BBC clock with its surprisingly loud tick, and the security guard or the cleaner, mop in hand, who always seemed to enter the studio as soon as the infamous red light was turned on. Because I have performed so regularly to a red light, it has become natural to me. Thus sometimes, when I'm very tired, I find it difficult to summon up the energy to 'really perform' without the adrenalin rush induced by an audience. When playing with orchestras that are not accustomed to performing with microphones, I have observed that some players get very nervous as soon as the red light goes on, and a few of them have admitted to me that they find playing in a recording studio more nerve-racking than performing in a concert. As with 'audience nerves', the more recordings you do, the more comfortable you will feel playing to a red light. However, the striking differences between these two performing genres may affect your outlook. For instance, if you make a mistake in a concert, it can be upsetting for you. Depending on the scale and importance of the mistake it may be upsetting for everyone else too – but no one will have died as a result of your error! (People do pass away during concerts, though, and often we have to continue to play. In this situation – while the St John Ambulance crew attend to the body – our lives, and our nerves, are put into perspective.)

If you make a mistake in a concert, it will be over relatively quickly and, I would hope, forgotten by the next day. On the other hand, an error on a CD, made in a recording studio, will be heard for generations to come.

> 'The gramophone seems to me a marvellous instrument.
> Moreover, it assures music of a complete
> and meticulous immortality.'
> Claude Debussy, 1862–1918

And so you had better put up your hand and request a re-take to get things exactly right.

Re-takes

When you make a mistake during a recording session, you should think to yourself: was it important? If it was an obvious error, the recording company will have spotted it and will cover the section again soon afterwards. If, however, it was a less noticeable slip, perhaps you should inform your principal player, who will ask the producer to do it again. If either the principal or the producer does not think it was important enough, leave it: there are many small mistakes that occur all the time, even in recordings, and you would be amazed what is and what is not heard in the 'recording box'. The combined sound of an orchestra is quite different from what any individual member hears. I have heard some players complain after listening from the audience. The balance seemed odd to them, but more than likely this was because they had become accustomed to a particular instrumental balance due to their position within the orchestra.

If you are a principal player and you wish to re-record a passage, then it may be worth waiting a little. When you are recording for CDs, there are many run-throughs followed by endless patching sessions. So you may find that the section in question will be covered once more anyway. But if it looks as though they are forging ahead regardless, and in your opinion it does need another attempt, speak clearly and say: 'Sorry, we need to do passage "X" again.' Don't 'um and err', just state what you want and no one should question it. Most importantly, before requesting a re-take:

- *Be certain that you can improve on your previous attempt and will not make the same mistake again.*

On the matter of recordings, the story springs to mind of a fine player who was highly conscientious, constantly going into 'the box' and telling the record producer about all the errors and little mistakes they had made. The recording company was very happy with this musician's playing and couldn't hear the majority of the errors. But they did request that that player should not perform in the next recording. This illustrates one of life's many quirks. If you tell enough people that you have made mistakes, or that you are not playing as well as you should, they may start believing you.

Never put yourself down, because people believe what they hear, especially if it's from the horse's mouth. It is a question of finding a balance between modesty and arrogance.

Linda Verrier

Nerves: the 'Virus'

• *Nerves are infectious. Never mention them!*
If there are only two pieces of advice you remember in this book, number one should be: 'Don't play other people's solos' (see the *Surviving in the Orchestral Profession* chapter). Number two should be: 'Never strike up a conversation about nerves just before a concert.' I have known so many players to be fine and dandy before a performance, myself included, when an inexperienced player has come bounding up like a puppy, and asked: 'How do you control your nerves because *I'm so nervous?*' or more often: 'Do *you* ever get nervous?' As soon as such remarks are made, the nerve virus will pass on to all those within earshot. Players who haven't felt the slightest flutter or shake for years will question their self-confidence, and if they go on to make a mistake, they will blame you.

A superb lead violinist came up to me recently after playing Roussel's Symphony No. 3 in G minor, a work with a virtuoso solo violin part. He had played absolutely beautifully but he was furious. The conductor for the performance had been a leader in the past, and, attempting empathy, he had told him moments before embarking on the symphony that this was the very piece which had haunted him throughout his playing career, and was in fact the work which had made him give up the violin. In a similar vein, a producer once sidled up to me while I was practising a fast flute solo. It was from a Dvořák symphony that we were to perform at a Promenade Concert that evening. 'The last person I heard play that passage totally screwed it up in the performance!' he said with a grin on his face. You have to be incredibly resilient to be able to brush off this sort of comment. Whether the intent is innocent or not, the nerve virus is definitely carried by such remarks.

A further illustration of how virulent it can be is the fact that at this moment I am in a car park, proof-reading this chapter, between a rehearsal and concert. Reading what I have written here, I have found my hands beginning to sweat and I am becoming slightly apprehensive about tonight's performance of Hindemith, Brahms and Strauss. I think I should stop now ...

Diet

It is always worth considering what you are eating just before a concert since this may affect how you feel at the time.

I have been fortunate. I have never suffered greatly from nerves throughout my career. Of course, I have occasionally had the 'shakes' and the odd sweaty palm, but I have never seized up during a concert – at least until a few years ago. During a concert in Hanley when we were performing a symphony by Duttileux (our orchestral assistant in those days pronounced it 'Dutty-lux'), I felt my whole chest tighten. I soldiered on; but after the concert I was so concerned with my physical constriction that I immediately tried to assess what might have been different in my life. All I could come up with was this. The month before, I had been given a cafetière for Christmas. I had been consuming extremely strong coffee at home, followed by my customary three 'wake-up' capuccinos before all performances. Cutting down on my caffeine intake seemed an obvious solution. But I've discovered since then that I do have a 'coffee intolerance'. So coffee had a doubly adverse effect on me.

Many musicians report that they suffer from such intolerance to different foods.

• *Check what you are eating just before your concerts, and note the effects.*

If you suffer from shaking, perhaps you should also refrain from consuming too much tea, coke and chocolate before a concert, as they also contain caffeine. It is worth noting that the brain can take up to twenty minutes to register how full you are. It is therefore easy (I know it from experience) to fill yourself up with a splendid curry before a gig and find, when you get on stage, that you are completely bloated, and unable to breathe or use your diaphragm properly until the second half of the concert.

Athletes analyse the food they eat in a scientific manner and musicians should do the same. The body and brain require great reserves of energy to pull them through each concert. However, the balance has to be perfect: eating too much will weigh them down and slow their responses, while eating too little may make them feel dizzy.

Drugs

'Beta-type receptor' sites are predominately situated in cells around the heart, although they are also present in vascular and other smooth muscles. When nervous, we produce extra adrenalin that stimulates these sites, and our nervous system in those areas becomes excited. There is a drug called a 'beta-blocker' (a beta-adrenergic blocking agent) that diminishes this activity, and reduces the heart's need for oxygen in addition to slowing the heartbeat down. It is prescribed to control high blood-pressure, coronary disease, hypertension and anxiety, although some musicians use the drug to help them steady their nerves and remain calm for performances. There are outstanding players I admire who either take beta-blockers regularly or take them occasionally for important solos. There are no data on the percentage of players who use them in the profession, as few people are willing to admit that they need drugs to perform.

For

Some people argue that if you have talent but are unable to deliver results because of your nerves, beta-blockers may give you the confidence to perform. It is widely known that some surgeons take beta-blockers to steady their hands during operations. You could conclude that, if *they* take them, it couldn't possibly be dangerous. However, just consider how many doctors smoke.

Against

Some sports ban the use of beta-blockers (archery, bowls and shooting, for example) and, while music shouldn't be equated with competitive sports, it is different from surgery which can be a matter of life and death. There are contrasting viewpoints on this complex issue.

It is important to note that beta-blockers were produced for specific health conditions. Taking them without medical consultation could be *life-threatening*. So:

• *Please get medical advice before taking anything of this kind.* If you are allowed to take them, you must remember that we don't know what the long-term effects of many drugs are. You must then decide which you think is worse: the long-term use of drugs or the long-term effect of the stress of performing on your body. No one can easily answer that.

You may be amazed to learn that beta-blockers are sometimes handed out by players to other players or, even worse, by teachers to students. This is an absolutely contemptible and unforgivable thing to do.

I have never taken this drug myself, so that I can only give you my reactions after observing the effects of beta-blockers on two players. It was not a scientific experiment, but the results are perhaps worth noting. In neither case did the player concerned shake. Both of them still had nerves and both felt that they were better equipped to combat their fears. However, while musician A played perfectly, it was with an extreme calmness that made their performance seem surreal and slightly dull. I knew in advance that this player was trying out the drug, and so perhaps my judgment was affected.

Player B appeared to be indifferent to the audience. Usually a dynamic soloist, this musician seemed to be performing with only two cylinders firing, and gave me the impression that they felt ill. I didn't know until afterwards that they had taken the drug.

Another point is that once you begin taking a drug, you may come to believe that you will never be able to play again without that crutch. It could be a vicious circle: you could become scared to stop taking it in case you lose control during performances, which could lead you to a negative attitude. You may start to believe that your reliance on it is an indication of your unsuitability for the profession. Be careful.

If you are seriously contemplating taking drugs – such as beta-blockers – to perform, I recommend that you also consider homeopathic equivalents such as gelsemium. But do seek the advice of a qualified homeopathic practitioner.

Alcohol

Having a swift drink to calm your nerves before a show may seem an innocent action; but for some it becomes a habit. I have witnessed players being sacked on the spot for wrecking a concert after drinking to excess. I personally don't trust myself with any amount of alcohol before playing in public. However, I see nothing wrong with people having a drink provided that their standard of playing is not adversely affected. You must remember that alcohol can deceive you: your brain may be convinced that finer playing would not have been possible for you, and yet, in reality, your motor-skills may have been totally unsynchronized. Players have been known to stagger on stage and attempt the highly skilled act of performing who would have been arrested if they had been caught driving a car.

Lucky Charms

Some soldiers carry amulets during combat, and some musicians admit to using a talisman to help them get through their performances. There is, of course, no scientific basis for lucky charms. All the same, the art of performing well is dependent on confidence. Whether you get the confidence you need by wearing a particular pair of lucky socks, or by practising until your socks fall off, is up to you! There are two players – I am mentioning no names, although they will know who they are – who swear by their lucky underwear.

Controlling Your Nerves Before the Performance

An Austrian man got into trouble recently for playing the flute in his car while driving. He was pulled over by the police after speeding through traffic at eighty mph on a busy highway. He had been steering with his knees while his hands were preoccupied with practising difficult finger-patterns. Maybe he should have heeded this advice:

Practise a long time in advance; never leave anything until the last minute; and aim to maintain a consistent standard so that there is no panic when an audition or important concert comes around.

Ben Hudson

When working at solo works or long orchestral passages, you should occasionally:

• *Perform during your practice.*

It is easy to become musically isolated while preparing for an important concert. Studying problem passages in minute detail and continually stopping to correct mistakes can lead to your losing sight of the grand picture and, with it, the ability to play from beginning to end. Play a work through without stopping, and pretend an audience is present. Observe the musical structure while feeling your heart beginning to race and your grip to tighten. In a concert, you don't have the luxury of a second attempt. So if your sound deteriorates in mid-phrase, endeavour to recover and bloom again without stopping. If you make a mistake, learn how to make a mental note without diminishing your concentration or interrupting the musical flow of the piece. Try and sound as polished, exciting and vibrant as you would in a concert. I have known players to turn the heat up in their house, or wear many layers of clothes, in an attempt to recreate the uncomfortable, clammy atmosphere one can experience when playing. I once cycled two miles on an exercise bicycle immediately before practising the flute solo from Debussy's *Prélude à l'après-midi d'un faune* in order to increase my heart-rate. If you think these are extreme measures, I must tell you of one player who used to perform concertos wearing shoes that were two sizes too small in the hope that this would distract him from his nerves.

• *One week before your next performance, or audition, ask a friend to listen to you.*

It doesn't matter if they are not a musician. Having *anybody* sitting in during a 'test-drive' of your performance will give you an idea of how you are going to feel on the big day. You may be surprised at the faults that you will make but don't be discouraged. These will highlight weaknesses you should focus on in the coming week.

• *Try to feel relaxed in the concert-hall environment.*

Imagine you are playing in the hall, and picture the audience sitting in front of you, full of anticipation. During rehearsals, and afterwards too, experience and experiment with the acoustics.

• *Take time out before you perform.*

> The way I get over my nerves is to prepare myself fully; although I don't do much practice on the day itself, and immediately beforehand I make sure that I'm in a quiet room on my own.
>
> Fiona Cross

In addition, you could try deep breathing as well as the Alexander technique or Yoga positions.

• *Try not to compare yourself with anyone else.*

Music is not a sport and although competition is inevitable, it doesn't improve creativity in a performance. Comparing yourself with other people will lead to negativity that may poison your mind and seep into your playing. You should be confident that you have something unique to offer.

Controlling Your Nerves During the Performance

• *Try to harness the energy that lies at the root of your nerves, and create excitement in place of fear.*

As long as you have done the required practice, you should realize that you will be doing as well as you possibly can. While performing, always:

• *Become deeply involved in the music and play for the composer.*

And occasionally:

• *Consciously scan your body for any undue muscle tension and then 'will' those areas to relax.*

An audience of 2,000 people can seem daunting, and so occasionally I pick out a handful of faces, and play for them.

• *Remember that confidence is the perfect antidote to stress and, like nerves, it is infectious.*

Feeling confident will not only enhance your performance but it can also stimulate other people to play better. I was always taught to act confidently on stage whether or not I was nervous.

• *Wondering what others may be thinking can lead to negative thoughts – and negative playing.*

'Your subconscious does not hear the word *don't*. So consider the implications of such a well-meaning instruction as "don't come in early", or how your brain perceives "I hope I don't screw up!"'

From *Performing Success: Performing Your Best Under Pressure*, by Don Greene, PhD

- *Making the odd slip is human and can sometimes be preferable to performing clinically.*

Such slips in a concert can easily faze the performer for a few seconds, and it takes great mental discipline to continue without faltering. Accept any mistake you make. Think positively, and relax, for at least you were trying.

- *Don't conduct any 'post-mortems' until after the concert.*

Learning from your faults is the quickest way of improving as you are your best teacher. However, too much self-criticism may make you play worse, as I have said.

- *Nobody likes seeing a sour face.*

Don't let anyone know that you have made an error from the expression on your face. Often, the only way that people can in fact tell that you are unhappy with your playing is when you frown or look angry.

Eventually, you should derive real enjoyment from a performance. When this happens, store it in your memory so that you can recall the experience at will. It may give you the confidence you need next time.

Still Nervous?

If you are constantly battling with your nerves, not just the reflex kind but the kind that causes vomiting and excessive shaking, perhaps you should talk things over with someone. Talking to an intelligent and sympathetic player, or maybe a doctor, will help, especially if nerves are ruining your life. While nerves can be paralysing, though, I feel that they shouldn't be the sole reason for quitting. You should attempt to look deeper, since other underlying problems may also need to be addressed.

Should You Give Up?

If, after taking all advice, you are still a bag of shaking bones when you perform or, more seriously, you have to take medication to get you through each performance, there may come a time when you should sit down and ask yourself whether thirty years of agony playing in the music profession really is the life for you. I have known many unhappy musicians who have pushed themselves hard through their careers: some of them good players, and some of them players who have lost or have been losing their skills through nerves.

- *Music should fundamentally be enjoyable. If it ceases to be fun, then perhaps you should stop playing.*

Towel in the Bidet

I often see candidates at auditions trying to suppress their nerves in a multitude of ways. Sometimes they mask their tensions successfully. But some applicants who are playing brilliantly suddenly break down and cry, saying that they can't possibly play another note as they are about to be sick. And sometimes musicians are so nervous that you can easily tell they would like the floor to open up and swallow them – and *you* too grip the sides of your chair in sympathy.

One of the most memorable stress-related stories I have to tell comes from when I was touring with the BBC. It was the first professional tour I had done, and it was a killer. Two gruelling weeks in Germany were followed by another two weeks in Italy. As we were a recording orchestra, programmes couldn't be repeated and we had to play different repertoire almost every night. The German half of the tour had come and gone smoothly, with pretty good concerts, hotels, food, and so on. Then we travelled to Italy by rail and people seemed to drop like flies with illness and upset stomachs. Breakfasts, which had previously been a glorious spread of mouth-watering meats, bread, yoghurt and eggs had shrunk to one crusty globule of bread and some watered-down orange juice. The breakfast bandits – players who steal enough food at breakfast to last them the whole day – were becoming despondent as they realized that they would have to start using up their expense allowance. Morale was plummeting. Friends were openly snapping at each other during rehearsals as a result of the strain; and yet we still had two weeks to go before the tour finished. The pressure was to be released in the most amazing water-fight across several balconies within a hotel's courtyard complex, the whole orchestra taking part in this stress-buster!

Before we reached this fever pitch, our first hotel in Italy had been on the outskirts of Modena. It was a large grey block of concrete beside a motorway, miles from civilization, by which I mean bars and restaurants. It had been chosen with good intentions as a base for us for three days: it enabled us to be transported to different venues. I had arranged to have the first concert in Italy off to give myself a breather and time to sample the local cuisine. Little did I know then that there weren't any local restaurants around. The day went by slowly; in fact time stood still. I spent it attending a 'dentist's-chair convention' that was being held in our hotel. You can imagine how much fun I had.

In the evening, I was waiting in the foyer for the orchestra to return when the orchestral assistant came rushing in, flustered. One of the extra string players on trial with us had attended the rehearsal during the day but had not turned up for the concert. By this point, the rest of the orchestral players had barricaded themselves in the bar area and were not going to be distracted at any price. Bored senseless by my attempt to pick out the most comfortable chair to sit in when having wisdom-teeth extracted, I offered to help her find out what had happened to the lost violist. We obtained his key and went to his room. We entered it and I half expected to find a body. In fact it was an empty room apart from a towel in the bidet. Later, I was told that the BBC then sent someone around to his London address who found him sitting with his feet up in front of an electric fire, drinking hot chocolate. Apparently he had just flipped and couldn't take any more.

> You mustn't get too flustered. This profession can be a bit pressurized and we all find it hard sometimes. Things go wrong. But you have to come back the next day and get on with it.
>
> Jonathan Goodall

For a more combative approach to conquering performance nerves, I recommend you to read the book I have mentioned, *Performance Success: Performing Your Best Under Pressure* by Don Greene, published by Routledge, which says this:

> 'Why not go out on a limb? Isn't that where the fruit is?'

Chapter 7

Counting

How to count the bars' rest

'Music is a kind of counting performed by the
mind without knowing it is counting.'
G.W. Leibniz, 1646–1716,
German philosopher, mathematician and political adviser

As an orchestral player, it is imperative that you should know
when to play. The most beautiful, expressive line played in the
wrong place is unacceptable. But does that mean that you must
endlessly count bars all day long? A student came to me recently
looking concerned. Baffled about the counting involved when
playing in a symphony orchestra, she asked me how I managed to
concentrate for so many hours each day, and was still able to play.
It was her first experience of playing in the college orchestra and
she was finding it mentally exhausting. Not only was she counting
emphatically but she was continually finding herself utterly lost,
which had led to regular emergency stops during her solos. My
reply was that I didn't concentrate on counting at all – Victoria,
my second-flute player, will vouch for that. The student seemed
taken aback at my response. The resulting discussion is the basis
for this chapter.

I told her how I was once taught by a famous flautist to use my
instrument like an abacus, and I use this method to this day when
I have more than a few bars' rest. Automatically depressing my
fingers in a set pattern on the 'down-beat' in each bar relieves me
of counting. All I have to do is look at the position of my fingers
to determine where I am in the music. That is the mechanical
method of counting, but for the majority of works it shouldn't
be necessary. When playing, you require an excellent sense of
musical direction, similar to that of a good map-reader – someone
who can always find where they are in an instant. If I am playing
a work I know very well, no counting will be involved at all
because I'm going on a familiar journey. No thought will be needed

about which route I should take. Identifying each junction and examining each sign-post will not be necessary. You simply enjoy the trip and arrive at your destination. The only time that further thought may be needed is when something unnerving happens. A dog may run in front of you, or perhaps a diversion may make you alter your approach – which is when your extra-sensory ensemble skills and different counting techniques will come into play. We'll deal with situations like that later in the chapter. Assuming nothing untoward does happen in the performance, if the music you are playing is in your blood, you will know when it is time to play. I consider that this is the best way to perform, if you can: no counting but just playing when it is musically the correct place to do so. Not long ago, this is what I said to a fellow musician, who raised her eyebrows. But I do find that the mathematics of counting can sometimes take over. Obsessive counting can mistakenly take priority over the flow of the music and you can easily catch yourself playing with as little expression as a sewing-machine. Counting can also become a reflex action. You may discover that you are doing it when you don't actually need to, and it has been known for players to miss their entrance totally, and yet continue to count religiously after they should have played.

Sometimes to relieve the boredom, you can play around with the larger numbers that you have to count. For example, 124 bars of rests can convert into 12 blocks of 10, plus 4. However, what happens if you forget which group of 10 you are on? We therefore need a back-up plan for all eventualities.

Look Out

- *In rehearsals you should keep a look-out for other players' cues and for notable key changes in the music, too.*

You need to be aware of when certain instruments come in and when others stop playing. Make a note of this. You mustn't be embarrassed about writing in obvious markings in your part as they may save your skin during the concert. In time, as you get to know the repertoire better, you will find that you won't have to do so much of this. You will soon become more aurally aware, and you may eventually find that you need a good-quality eraser in rehearsals rather than a pencil. I'm often surprised when I look through my old parts in the orchestral library. They seem to be full of 'unnecessary' markings. All the same, in their day they were my life-lines.

The Domino Factor

You must be flexible in your counting strategy as you may be waiting for a particular solo or cue that for some reason doesn't materialize. One player's momentary lack of concentration can trip up an entire orchestra. This is 'the domino factor'. A player's mind wanders just for an instant; they slip up by missing an entry or by playing it in the wrong place; and the first domino topples. That entry may have been a cue for several people. The confusion spreads and other musicians stumble. Note-mistakes and mis-entries appear from all directions in a cascade.

I have been in a situation when I could hear dominoes toppling all around me and I knew that it would soon be my turn. I was determined not to succumb ... but you have to be strong to resist the domino factor. You often hear, when you leave the stage: 'ah yes ... but the reason I didn't play ... was ... because ... um ... I was waiting for that ... you know ... trombone bit.'

Let us look at some counting strategies to enable you to find your way back on course.

Counting Strategies

If you are a string player, counting endless empty bars is not the problem it is for the brass, woodwind and percussion sections. First, the strings play for much longer periods of time and there are few empty bars for them to count. More important, they share the same music. For the majority of the repertoire, all strings play identical parts in their section and two musicians share a music stand. (See the quote from *Philharmonic* in the 'Count Upwards' section later on in this chapter, page 139.) If one of them gets lost in the middle of a performance, listening to their neighbour will help them find the right place. In the other sections of the orchestra, however, each player has their own stand, with separate music containing different notes and special rhythms. If they get lost, they are on their own.

What Do You Do?

If someone plays an entry that you feel is in the wrong place, you have to think fast. The 'self-doubting' side of your personality may assume that it is *you* who have miscounted or skipped a line, while the 'confident side' may think that *they* have miscounted. Who is right?

Sounds Wrong?

If the entry in question sounds very wrong, then you can take it that you were right all along. However, watch out for musical tricks such as the false horn entry before the recapitulation in the first movement of Beethoven's *Eroica* Symphony (see facing page).

It caused a critic at the time to accuse the second horn player of miscounting. This is why you should write down your observations in your part during rehearsals.

Sounds Right?

If the entry concerned comes in a bar or so late, or early, in your system of counting but sounds right, don't query it. Assume that you were the guilty one, and see what happens next.

Not Sure?

By this time, you will have checked that you didn't skip a line. If you are still not sure who was right and who was wrong, then you may have to continue counting, this time on two levels. For example: bar 34 or 35 ... 2 ... 3 ... 4 ... bar 35 or 36 ... 2 ... 3 ... 4 ... With luck something obvious will soon indicate where you should be.

• *Get your musical compass out and listen for landmarks and sign-posts. If you spot one, latch on to it.*

Often a player close to you will notice the confusion and take the initiative by playing confidently, thus enabling you to follow them. If possible, it will all happen and become sorted out within seconds, before any more mis-entries occur.

Beethoven, *Eroica*, 1st movement

Asking for Help

Musicians are sensitive creatures. If you turn slightly towards your neighbour, they will probably show you where they are in the music by mouthing the bar-number, or else they may indicate the next big rehearsal figure by tapping their knee. This is common practice. You don't need to respond. You can thank them after the concert.

I have never known a player give a wrong bar number on purpose, but it can happen by mistake. So watch out for the two commonest problems when you ask for help. You may discover that the player you have asked is also confused, and therefore taking their advice would be disastrous. But if the player is in the correct place, there is still a potential problem. They may have a different number of bars to count, or their bars may be grouped in a different way. If they whisper confidently that they are on bar 132 when you are expecting a number in the low 20s, the confusion will be compounded. In such a situation you may have to look briefly over at their music while simultaneously counting on two tiers, and then start applying school mental arithmetic to find out where you should be.

Still Lost?

If you find that you are lost just before a solo, you will have to follow your instinct. You may choose to enter rather discreetly in case you are still wrong, and then you can always add a musical crescendo if or when you are absolutely sure you are in the right place. For 99% of the time you will find that a combination of these pieces of advice will get you out of trouble and put you back on track seamlessly. But if your intuition fails you, if no one near by has the foggiest idea of where they are – it does happen – and if there is a big solo coming up, then you need to go into emergency mode.

Emergency Mode

Put your instrument in its playing position and open your eyes wide in a panic-stricken way as if to say 'Help!' Unless he is sculpturing the air with his eyes shut, the conductor, who should be clairvoyant, will observe this and bring you in correctly.

Count Upwards

Another tip is always to count upwards i.e. 1 bar ... 2 bars ... 3 bars ... Play, and never *downwards*. Logically, you can do either, but I am reminded of the novel called *Philharmonic* by Herbert Russcol and Margalit Banai, which predates Jilly Cooper's *Appassionata* by over twenty years. Both books explore the antics and rigours of orchestral life in a semi-fictional way. The former is loosely based on the Boston Symphony Orchestra, and although the authors deny this in the foreword, it is easy to identify eminent players and conductors who have been associated with that orchestra. A rank and file 'cellist, Stephan Graesler, incurs the wrath of the tyrannical but fictitious conductor, Paul Klange. The maestro has been targeting Stephan for some time, singling him out in rehearsals, and making him play passages on his own and then calling him 'a shoe-maker' in front of his colleagues. When he remarks that the day Stephan was born was a black day for music, you realize that a firing is imminent. Towards the end of the book, Stephan's neurotic fears over a passage in Berlioz's *Symphonie Fantastique* are acutely pertinent to many musicians. Over four intense pages, the authors get inside Stephan's mind during the concert as he counts *down* the bars towards what is to be his nemesis. Each paragraph is equal to a bar, although in this extract, I have made some cuts. The tempo is fast and it is conducted 'two in a bar'.

'It was the feverish, nightmarish March that the 'cellist Stephan Graesler awaited with special dread ... The oboes, flutes, bassoons and clarinets shrieked and danced along in the March to the Scaffold. They sounded magnificent. Graesler had always been jealous of wind players. Each had their own individual part to play; they weren't all locked in a chain gang as he was, condemned to sawing away at the same music that all the other eleven 'cellos played. It made him feel like a galley slave ... Six (bars to go) ... The passage was coming soon, he had better be right in his counting ... Five. His palms were wet ... Four. Keep calm, don't get excited, don't make Klange suffer. Not to-night. Nothing must go wrong ... Three. He felt the beads of sweat break out on his glistening bald head ... Two ... here we go now ... Klange veered, crouching low on the podium, and cued the 'cellos into the March to the Scaffold ... like Stephan Graesler's own garrotter, beckoning him to join the dance of death ... (One) ... Stephan Graesler attacked the music – splendidly, decisively ...

[... but all on his own! He was a bar too early, because if you count downwards, you should play on bar 0, not on bar 1! Stephan commits suicide after the concert.]

From *Philharmonic* by Herbert Russcol and Margalit Banai.

(Reprinted by permission of PFD on behalf of
Herbert Russcol and Margalit Banai.

© Herbert Russcol and Margalit Banai, as per original edition)

Complex Music Shouldn't Mean Complicated Counting

If you get lost in a work that changes time frequently, it should be easy to watch out for particular conducting patterns. Traditionally trained conductors have 'geographically-identifiable' beats so that experienced orchestral musicians will be able to look up at any time – whether they are lost or merely want clarification – and recognize the bar's length, and exactly where they are within that bar, solely from the position and trajectory of the conductor's hands. For example, often when I have a variety of bar-lengths before a 4/4 bar, I just relax, watch the conductor and wait for a clear 4/4 bar to materialize. Choose wisely, though, if you are going to use this method as it only works if you have a reliable and clear conductor (see the next chapter).

A famous English conductor was once conducting a modern work that had some time-changes that were difficult for people to count. In the dress rehearsal, he told the orchestra that the piece was like a fair-ground carousel and that they would have to concentrate hard that evening. If any of them were to fall off, he couldn't guarantee that he could get them back on again.

You Are Not Alone

Musicians do regularly get lost during performances. So you are not alone. The most important thing is to *know* that you are lost. I have known players not to notice that they are in the wrong place and continue for line after line before grinding the orchestra to a halt. To change the subject, I remember playing in a concert with a semi-professional orchestra when a clarinettist performed a whole slow movement on the wrong clarinet. He played a semitone higher than everyone else throughout and didn't notice anything was wrong – only that the whole band was doubled up with laughter for some reason.

Once you are lost, the real skill is to recover quickly without the listener noticing. These things go on all the time, as I say, and you have to be cool and flexible, and make split-second decisions. I know of fabulous players who can't count for toffee and go through every performance on the edge of their seat so that they are ready to play when the conductor gives them their cue. There are others who only feel comfortable when they have studied the full score in its entirety and know when to play from the overall musical context. You must find your own way of coping with the problem of counting. Experience will help. You will in time feel more relaxed and eventually be able to play musically while counting at the same time.

Lost Souls

On one occasion, two flautists were playing along in a concert and the second was lost. He turned to the first and asked: 'Where are we?' The first put down his flute, turned to him and whispered: 'The Royal Albert Hall.'

Every musician has many counting stories to relate: some of them hilarious and others which will make you cringe with embarrassment. We have played concertos when even the soloist has lost their place and the orchestra has had to skip forwards some bars automatically to catch up. Once, when this happened, the soloist realized what he had done and corrected the error a few bars later, forcing us to skip back again. There was relief on the soloist's face at the end of the performance. With a furtive glance, he scanned the orchestra anxiously to see whether anyone had noticed his momentary blunder. He had no inkling that we had skipped around and followed him in a game of musical hopscotch.

One of my favourite stories, familiar to many, comes from a European orchestra, one of the world's greatest. They were touring the USA when, towards the end of the trip, their percussionist fell ill. Usually, orchestras in this situation hire a local player to remedy their misfortune but not this elite band. They decided that none of the East Coast orchestras in America had a percussionist who could quite fit their requirements in their final concert, and felt it was imperative to fly over an extra player from Europe. The only work for which he was required was Bruckner's Seventh Symphony. In this enormous piece, there is just one cymbal note for the percussionist in the whole work. No rhythmical side-drum, no triangle trill. All he had to do was count and crash. That's it – nothing else. They flew him over and he arrived just in time for the concert. Whether it was jet-lag or too much complimentary in-flight beverage nobody knows, but as the symphony dragged on and he waited for his moment of glory, he gently drifted off to sleep. He missed his entry. He slept right through the rest of the concert and flew back home the following day without having played a single note.

In this chapter, we have examined a range of methods to help you keep your place in the music and pinpoint when you should next play. Once you can do this, your ensemble skills will have to take over and assess in which *thousandth* of a second you should actually start playing your note. However, how can we play together with colleagues sitting fifty feet away, and how can we interpret the conductor's beat in such a way that all ninety of us play simultaneously?

Chapter 8

Conductors

including when to play

> 'There are no good or bad orchestras,
> only good or bad conductors.'
> Traditional

Every orchestra has its own 'time-zone' that it operates within: that is, the period between the conductor's baton coming down and the players' response and creation of sound. On occasion, this time-lag can seem an eternity. The final chord of a slow movement can have everyone waiting on tenterhooks as they make sure they do not commit one of the worst crimes in the orchestral business: playing before anyone else. To do the opposite is also a sin, for if you are heard after everyone has stopped, even for a split second, you are equally guilty. (See 'Note-Endings' in the *Ensemble* chapter, on page 93.) The conductor may bring his baton down very gently, cushioning it to make sure no one comes in with too much of an accent. Hearing nothing, he may even have to produce another little beat – and then wait. I've seen conductors laugh at the delay before the flooding out of lush, velvety sound. Sometimes one gets a conductor who insists that everybody plays exactly in time with the beat. This may at first seem logical until you become aware of the light/sound speed-ratio I will describe. Any orchestral musician will tell you that if such a request is followed through literally, it will lead to failure. The reality is that all orchestras throughout the world respond differently to the beat of a maestro, and so indeed do the individual sections within each orchestra. This is because of the distance between the players, together with the fact that sound travels relatively slowly, at around 330 metres per second, compared to the light that enables us to see, which travels at nearly 300 million metres per second. That means that sound from your instrument travels over nine hundred thousand times more slowly than the light-waves by means of which the conductor's beat reaches your eyes. If all the players were to interpret the beat identically, the sounds from them would reach the conductor at slightly different times, and so each section has to compensate differently for the time-lag. An experienced ensemble will take this phenomenon into account, observing the gesticulations of the conductor, and measuring up the distance he is away, whilst allowing for both articulation and the acoustics, with the aim of sounding together.

> 'There is a time-lag of one fifth of a second
> per fifty feet – allow for it.'
> Sir Henry Wood, conductor, 1869–1944

The Player's Wish: A Clear Up-Beat

to be read by aspiring conductors

If we put the interpretative, inspirational and educational aspects of conducting to one side, and ignore the mechanics of cueing entries, what orchestral players desire most is a clear 'up-beat'. Very little else is required for an ensemble to play together, provided that you know when your instrument is going to respond (see the next section). I have come across conductors who have played jokes, giving the orchestra a crystal clear up-beat (the speed at which the arm is raised) and no following down-beat at all – to illustrate that the band will still sound together. I have tried this myself when conducting ensembles, and it does work as long as the up-beat is clear.

> 'Breathe together before the attack! Watch my stick:
> it shows you when to take breath for the chord.'
> Sir Henry Wood

These exhortations were regularly made at Sir Henry's rehearsals. All sections, not just the wind-players, were to breathe with his up-beat, and to understand that the secret of clarity in attack lay in the preparation of his beat.

Orchestral musicians observe the up-beat and they assume that the following down-beat will be at the same speed. This vital, all-important movement indicates in advance what the tempo of the next bar, or section, or accelerando, etc, will be. As a team-player, one has to know exactly when to play so that the sound is projected uniformly. The preparation for one's note has to be executed a millisecond before it sounds and this can only be done if the player is lucid and absolutely confident of when to play. Any confusion whatever will result in frayed and tattered playing. An unambiguous up-beat allows him to calculate these things, and when the down-beat does materialize, it then clarifies the situation. This is by no means the only way to direct an orchestra successfully. There are some conductors who conjure up extremely tight performances following their own methods – perhaps using an eyebrow to bring in an entire brass section with such ensemble perfection it would make you weep. But they are magicians and this article is not for or about them. When conductors do follow the clear up-beat principle, it makes pinpointing the precise moment of when to play easy, even if there is no down-beat at all. Problems only arise if the resulting down-beat is faster or slower. For an orchestral musician, the up-beat is like having a ball thrown up in the air. By judging a ball's speed and trajectory, it is easy to predict where your hands would have to be to catch it. If gravity were to play a trick on you, maybe bringing the ball down more quickly than you expected, you would fail to catch it, or at least stumble. Incompetent conductors may be at a loss as they wonder why orchestras are so difficult to get to sound together. In reality, it is often they themselves who are causing the problems. Regularly throwing 'trick balls' for us to catch, their up-beat may bear little relation to the down-beat that follows. The players then have to scramble to catch the beat as it bounces around uncontrollably.

I'm not recommending rigidity in beating but the achievement of clarity in what is about to happen. Beecham was a master at bringing in chords a split-second early, and so creating drama. But this requires instinctive calculation and an additional flick in the up-beat that will be interpreted in the correct manner. If such a move is executed perfectly, the audience will be thrilled. Otherwise it is the orchestra that will be plunged into drama.

A conductor's innate physical coordination and his ability to convey his intentions to the orchestra will be even more important when tempo changes occur in a work. If he is clear a fraction of a second before a tempo change, everything will fall into place. If he is uncoordinated or has doubts about the relationship between sections, chaos will ensue. (Read the 'Learn to Conduct' section of the *Performing Philosophies* chapter, on page 46.) It may astonish the reader to know that occasionally a conductor will have such a phobia about a tempo change in a recording session that the only way for him to produce a good result is by recording the relevant passages separately, each at a different speed, and leave the recording engineers to cut, splice and patch them together. A genuine conductor should be able to lead the orchestra through the roughest terrain, making transitions effortless, and still exhilarating the listener.

I have mentioned 'magician' conductors who sometimes use their shoulders or eyebrows, or other parts of their bodies, to create effects, paint musical landscapes and establish ensemble. Such seemingly eccentric gestures may not be as bizarre as you may think since they send the players a signal: they are given the freedom to listen. All too often, a severe beat will have the effect of deafening players, robbing them of their musical instincts, and compelling them to rely purely on sight. Given the opportunity, musicians *will play together.*

Do You Know Exactly When You Are About to Play?

One of the most important steps in interpreting the maestro's beat is to make sure that your own note 'sounds' when *you* want it to. If it doesn't, you won't be able to play in an orchestra just yet.

Close your eyes when undertaking the following exercise so that you can focus without distraction. Imagine a graceful up-beat, and envisage the moment when the note will sound together with the resulting down-beat. Prepare and attempt to play at exactly this point in space and time. Did the note sound when you expected it to? One *thousandth* of a second either way will not be acceptable. Try with different speeds for the up-beat, vary the dynamics and use a multitude of different attacks. If it is difficult for you to visualize a conductor's beat, set your metronome to a slow pulse instead – but still close your eyes. Once you are in control of your own note-beginnings, you are well on the way to interpreting the conductor's technique.

As a newcomer to the profession, you will have to listen to each different orchestra's response to a conductor and quickly adapt to the time difference you perceive.

You have to distinguish between when you are leading and when you are following. If you are playing a second or third part in the wind or brass sections, or if you are a rank and file string player, then most of the time you will be following someone else. The difficulty for them is to learn where and when to place their line in relation to what everyone else is doing. We have the problem of sitting forty or fifty feet away from some of our colleagues, and so occasionally I have to play in a way that will give them something to follow.

Patrick Addinall

- *'Tripping up' another player by entering a split-second too early is much worse than playing a split-second late.*

Playing exactly together with everyone else is of course what we should be aiming for, but:

> If someone were to come in a little early, that might undermine my coordination and make me miss the note I was preparing to play.

Patrick Addinall

An exceptional, natural conductor rehearsing our orchestra a few years ago said this:

> 'It is the player's crime to play early and the conductor's crime if you play late!'

Gennadi Rozhdestvensky, b.1931,
Russian conductor

Upsetting the Apple Cart

Insensitive ensemble players will be unaware of the havoc they create. They may notice, however, that wherever they play, the ensemble will be ragged and musicians will seem to topple off notes regularly.

> People coming in slightly early because they aren't listening to the other parts is one of the things that I really listen out for. In the 'cellos, we obviously interact constantly with the violins and violas. For example, in Brahms's Fourth Symphony we have a dotted quaver and semi-quaver pattern that is repeated whilst the rest of the strings have constant running semi-quavers. Someone who jumps the gun when there is such an obvious semi-quaver pulse going on just ten feet away, has to go because they will trip up the whole section. If they were sitting at the back doing this, you would be aware that something was not quite right. You might think that another problem had developed, but it's amazing how often that it will be them who are

upsetting the 'apple cart'. If one person comes in slightly early, then the other nine will just not know when to play. It is as disconcerting as when you have a conductor who can't keep time properly: you look up, expecting to see a down-beat, and they're still at the end of the up-beat.

Peter Dixon

What Difference Do Conductors Make?

One of the most frequently asked questions from the public is: what difference does a conductor *really* make to the end product? The first time I experienced playing with a top-flight maestro, my eyes were opened to the extremes to be found in the conducting profession. The previous night, we had played a concert with a good, solid conductor. The ensemble had been fine and the concert had gone pretty well, but with this eminent talent conducting us the next day, the difference was remarkable. Every single person played with commitment, the standard was breathtaking, and a Saturday morning rehearsal became one of the most moving experiences of my life.

The simple answer to the question is: a good conductor will make you play well. As long as they don't get in the way too much, a performance with a mediocre conductor may also be good, although there may be a few ragged edges. An outstanding conductor, on the other hand, will nourish the ensemble, enrich the soul and elevate the art of performing and interpreting orchestral music to the heights it deserves.

The complete conductor will optimize rehearsals by wasting little time verbalizing their interpretation. A true maestro will convey musical thoughts solely through body language using their innate coordination, their intellect and their understanding to absorb *all* the musicians into their musical vision – producing art without effort.

Bad Conductors

Bad conductors are another matter altogether. They are abundant and cause orchestral musicians more grief than they ever realize. A bad conductor is like a poor ensemble player. They trip up

148

musicians, too, creating confusion, and, rather than affecting only a handful of players, they affect everyone.

In Bernard Shore's *The Orchestra Speaks*, written in 1938, there is a true story about a conductor directing a London theatre orchestra who was so incompetent with his up-beat that he couldn't even get the orchestra to play without the leader's help. The leader had to indicate tempo changes with his violin, and cue all the players in at the right moment, whenever this conductor took to the podium. One day, the leader was taken ill and a deputy took his place. The conductor raised his stick in the usual way; everyone got into their playing positions; the tension grew; but nothing happened. With a pained expression, he lowered his baton and everyone relaxed. Once more he raised his arms, and once more the guest leader set the bow to his violin and looked up at him for a signal to play. After another long pause, the conductor turned to him and hissed: 'For heaven's sake, man, what are you waiting for?'

Why We Need Them

With so many players on stage, such complex music to be performed and finite rehearsal time available, democracy can play no part in orchestral life. The conductor is in reality essential for clear direction and for interpretation of the music, as well as for educating and motivating people. However, finding a maestro with all these qualities is extremely difficult.

> When you come into this profession, you don't expect to earn a lot of money, but what you do expect is to have some sort of artistic fulfilment. I got quite depressed a while ago about the standard of conductors. When they are bad, it highlights how unfulfilling the job can be. A conductor should be able to stand on the podium and display a knowledge that is greater than that of everyone else in the orchestra, but so often they have nothing to offer.
>
> Miriam Skinner

Where Did They Come From?

The violinist-composer-conductor Louis Spohr produced the first baton at a rehearsal in 1820, much to the disapproval of the

London orchestra he was directing. He appears to have moved towards using this method after being asked by some singers three years earlier to abandon his customary waving of a rolled-up manuscript. The alternative method at the time was to lead the orchestra while playing the violin and occasionally use the bow to direct it. At the singers' request, he attempted this but – finding it unnatural – laid down his instrument immediately and began to use his bow as a baton exclusively.

As far back as the fifteenth century, the choir of the Sistine Chapel had also kept their performances in time by means of a director who waved a roll of paper. It was the custom then to slap the tube audibly in order to maintain a steady beat, and although variations of this 'paper-baton' method seem to have been practised for the next four hundred years, other ways of conducting wove in and out of fashion as well. For a while, requiring the composer to thud a large pole against the floor was popular although that method was abandoned when the noise became too intrusive – and when news was received of Lully's death in 1687. Jean-Baptiste Lully, the Italian-born composer, had stabbed his foot with such a pole while directing an orchestra, and the resulting gangrenous infection had proved fatal.

Directing from the keyboard was to become popular with Mozart and Haydn, but one thing remained constant throughout the centuries: the directing role was exclusively taken by composers and violinists since no conducting profession existed. As the music of the nineteenth century became more complicated, new demands arose. Innovative methods of conducting had to be developed in order to control and balance the large orchestras the music of the era required. Having so many musicians on stage playing a new style of music that often incorporated a multitude of tempo changes posed problems of ensemble that needed to be addressed. Composers were also beginning to insist on a single interpretative viewpoint so that new techniques and codes had to be invented. Composers like Berlioz and Wagner were to write treatises on different techniques for conducting. Soon afterwards, the professional conductor was born.

A good modern conductor needs musical vision, an authoritative sensibility, physical coordination and unassailable leadership. Orchestral boards are also keen for conductors to have a magnetic personality that can be harnessed for public relations purposes, for attracting audiences and revenue.

The more famous conductors today command pop-star fees and grace the covers of music magazines. This elevated status can sometimes lead to arrogance, and the tyrannical outbursts of many of them are well documented. Inevitably, conductors will pick on you personally from time to time, but don't let this intimidate you. The great ones won't rip you to shreds. They will encourage you and help you reach musical heights you thought were unattainable. It is the mediocre conductors, who lack skill, and are not able to communicate through the art of conducting, who will try to make you feel inadequate for not playing the way they wish. You have to acquire a pretty thick skin for those times when a conductor turns nasty, or decides to 'nit-pick'. If they know what they are talking about, they can be enlightening. But often they are amateur sailors, steering majestic vessels in busy shipping-lanes.

It is always worth remaining dignified when talking across the orchestra to conductors:

> I have lost my rag on a few occasions, but I have found that it is quite hard to play afterwards, so I have learnt from experience that it is best to just quietly get on with it. You stand a better chance of getting your own way if you keep on an even keel.
>
> Jonathan Goodall

Conductors' Traits

> Nerves are a negligible problem for me if I've got a conductor on the box that I can trust, and as long as I've done enough of what fiddle players call 'right-arm preparation'. You need to know where you are in the bow at any given time. What can rattle you is when a conductor goes off at a tangent and therefore, technically, you're not quite in the right spot at the right time. This can happen as easy as pie, just by the conductor being erratic.
>
> Robert Chasey

Be prepared for conductors to get excited from time to time. Their rehearsal tempo may differ significantly from their concert tempo – usually the latter will be faster when they become excited and slower when they are emotionally moved. When practising, you may want to vary the tempo by 20% each way as an insurance policy so that your fingers/tongue/bow don't get in a tangle during the performance.

> 'A conductor should reconcile himself to the
> realization that regardless of his approach or temperament
> the eventual result is the same – the orchestra will hate him!'
> Oscar Levant,
> American composer, 1906–72

How to Cook a Conductor has appeared all over the world on orchestral notice-boards. This anonymously written article illustrates the strength of feeling musicians have towards bad conductors.

How to Cook a Conductor

Ingredients
One large Conductor, or two small assistant conductors
Ketchup
26 large garlic cloves
Crisco or other solid vegetable shortening (lard may be used)
1 cask cheap wine
1 lb alfalfa sprouts
2 lb assorted yuppie food, such as tofu or yoghurt
One abused Orchestra

First, catch a Conductor. Remove the tail and horns. Carefully separate the large ego and reserve for sauce. Remove any batons, pencils (on permanent loan from the Principal Second Violin) and discard. Remove the hearing aid – it never worked anyway. Examine your Conductor carefully – many of them are mostly large intestine. If you have such a Conductor, you will have to discard it and catch another. Clean the Conductor as you would a squid, but do not separate the tentacles from the body. If you have an older Conductor, such as one from a Major Symphony Orchestra or Summer Music Festival, you may wish to tenderize by pounding the Conductor on a rock with timpani mallets or by smashing the Conductor between two large cymbals.

Next, pour ½ of the cask of wine into a bath tub and soak the Conductor in the wine for at least 12 hours (exceptions: British, German and some Canadian Conductors have a natural beery taste which some people like and the wine might not marry well with this flavour. Use your judgment). Make a sauce by combining the ego, sprouts and ketchup to taste, placing it all in the blender and pureeing until smooth. If the ego is bitter, sweeten with honey to taste. When the Conductor is sufficiently marinated, remove any clothes the Conductor may be wearing and rub it all over with the garlic.

Be careful not to overcook or your Conductor could end up tasting like stuffed ham. Slice your Conductor as you would any turkey.

The Baton Makes No Sound

Conductors sporadically make mistakes although few will admit it. If this happens during a rehearsal, it's harmless enough. But look out for this common excuse: 'Oh, I'm glad we've stopped because I wanted to sort out some bowings in the violas,' rather than 'Whoops, sorry everybody!' If, however, a conductor makes an error in a concert, then it is a more serious matter. Often musicians will be left vulnerable and open to criticism, and so we do have to know when to follow conductors and when to ignore them. Having got to know your conductor well is a boon for if they are infamously unreliable, you will be more inclined to ignore their leads. (See the *Counting* chapter to make sure you know where you are, though.)

> Orchestras are very good at disguising bad conductors: they can bale them out of almost anything.
>
> David Fanning

On one occasion, I had the fiercest of glares from a conductor who gave me a lead which I knew to be wrong and had to ignore. He then signalled to me again to play, scowling viciously. Once more, I did not play. It was during a cadenza in a 'cello concerto. Not only did I know it well but I also had the soloist's line clearly cued in in my part. I could see exactly where I was. If I hadn't had this extra crutch, I would possibly have followed the conductor. I had to make an executive decision in a split-second. I decided to follow my cue, and came in where I thought it was right, accompanied by much congratulatory shuffling from the orchestra. Although I considered my decision to have been the right one musically, the conductor continued to glare at me, on and off, throughout the rest of the evening. Perhaps this was because I had shown him up. But if I had come in when he indicated, I would have had a host of glares from the soloist, the orchestra and the audience, to say nothing of a bad write-up in the papers the next day.

Another conducting nightmare which still haunts me is an experience I had during my first live television broadcast, when I was in the band that accompanied the finals of the Leeds International Piano Competition. I was still at college and very wet behind the ears. The problem again was the link between the cadenza and coda of a concerto …

Perhaps we hadn't had enough rehearsal time. Anyhow, half the orchestra interpreted the conductor's beat as indicating a full bar before they played, and the other half thought it was merely an up-beat into the final section. For what seemed an eternity, the two halves of the orchestra were half a bar out from each other in one of the best known concertos of all time. It was my first playing of this work and, although I had heard it before, I had never heard this dissonant version and so didn't know which half of the orchestra to play with. I'd like to think that I would have been able to link up with the right half today. But who knows? It is interesting to note that many conductors, even good ones, find accompanying concertos incredibly tricky. Either they can't accept that there is a different interpretation from their own or perhaps a primeval instinct emerges: the ego. As orchestral players, we witness many arguments between soloists and conductors as they battle to establish the superiority of their own interpretation.

There Are Wonderful Conductors, Too

When you play for an exceptional conductor, there are *no* problems. The few of them on this planet are a precious commodity, as I have said, and in great demand with orchestras, who long for them to visit. Musicians know that when playing for such conductors, the ensemble will be tight and the performance ecstatic. In your career, you will play many different interpretations of a work as nothing is 'set in stone'. There is no single way of playing a piece but a great conductor will make you feel *his* interpretation is 'the one'. Everything will simply fit into the 'right' place as he mesmerizes you into playing well, shaping his vision naturally, with little talk. It is rare, but it can happen.

When to Play, a Possible Answer

Soon after my appointment, a brass player who was close to retirement told me the following tale. He was once hired to play principal trombone with the Hallé in the days of Barbirolli. It was an emergency and he had missed the rehearsal; indeed he only just made it to the concert. I don't remember what the first piece was he said they were playing, solely that it had a big brass chord at the beginning. He was used to playing very close to the beat, and so he thundered in 'blastissimo' when the great man brought his baton down. He found he was playing completely on his own: 'soloistico embarrassato'. I can imagine the cacophonous sound. He was totally confused throughout the piece as the conductor's beat seemed to bear no relation to the way the musicians were placing their notes. Eventually, when they got to the end, a colleague leant over and said in a broad Lancashire accent: 'Eh, lad, you never play with ah John's beat. You've got to wait for his forelock to fall on t'his eyebrows before blowin' in loud bits, and for his stick to reach second t'last button of his waistcoat for quieter passages.'

Chapter 9

Intonation

'Notes of sorrow out of tune are worse
Than priests and fanes that lie.'
William Shakespeare, *Cymbeline*

Intonation is a contentious subject. Merely mentioning the matter of playing in tune can make the most hardened musicians defensive and hot under the collar.

'Wrong notes we may admit, poor phrasing possibly,
bad ensemble, yes; but out of tune – never!'
From Where I Sit
Jack Brymer, British clarinettist, 1915–2003

The ability to play in tune is of paramount importance for working in any ensemble.

It is our number-one requirement. Whoever comes into our orchestra has to possess a really good ear and be able to play their instrument *in tune*. Once that has been established, you can start to pile other things on top such as clean articulation, good sound variation, and so on. It has to be said there are many who come for auditions whose ears are lacking – I don't think they've ever been told that you actually have to listen and analyse every single thing you play.

Robert Chasey

Imagine asking someone to retain a mental picture of a specific paint colour in order to cover a patch on a wall. You require the match to be exact so that the new paint blends imperceptibly with the old. The slightest shade difference will be unacceptable to most people and yet almost everybody faced with this test will fail to pick out the exact tint from the millions available. This gives an idea of how important intonation is to the musician. The sound you produce has to be beautiful, the articulation appropriate and the blend of intonation exact.

Our struggle to play in tune with other musicians is discussed later in this chapter. First of all we need some history, some mathematics and some science lessons to point us in new directions to open up our minds and ears to the vast array of possibilities. How detailed should our analysis be? While researching the subject of intonation, I soon found that it became far too complex for what I am intending to achieve in this book. What I want to do is to deal with what is possible in an orchestral context without our losing our way in a black hole of acoustical science. For a while, I considered brushing past the subject, or perhaps omitting it completely. Although that might have been wise, I came to feel that an ensemble guide failing to tackle the problems of intonation would be inadequate. I hope that the following information will not only educate you generally but also unlock fresh tuning terrain for you to explore. If you find the next few pages heavy-going, skip through to the 'Practical Experiment', on page 174, since this is vital if you are to awaken your equal-tempered and sanitized ears to a truer pitch for all.

Science Lesson

With intonation, Mother Nature has set us a real conundrum. Clues to unravelling the problem are given in different sections in the chapter so that you can begin to comprehend and digest its complexity. Let us first look closer at our hearing faculty which determines how we label pitch and recognize different instruments.

Hearing

I described in the 'Dynamics' section of the *Ensemble* chapter (page 108) how there are thousands of hair-cells on the cochlea in the inner ear that vibrate in accordance with how loudly a note is being played. These hair-cells are used for intonation, too. There are hair-cells that at one end of the cochlea only respond to high notes, and at the other to low ones. The hairs send electrical signals from the inner ear through a nerve up to the brain for it to interpret, and to enable it to establish pitch (by judging which ones are vibrating) and dynamics (by the vigour of that vibration). How do we perceive which instrument is playing? From the information it receives, the brain is also able to decipher which instrument you are listening to by breaking down the harmonics within the sound that is being heard.

Natural Harmonics

Within any tone played by any orchestral instrument, Nature has added a particular mixture of harmonics or partials that colour the note from the inside. These are almost universal and follow a similar pattern. An exception is the clarinet which has a cylindrically-stopped tube (see 'The Clarinet Problem' on page 199). The player's lips cover (or stop) the tube and alter the sound-wave within it. As a result, it sounds an octave lower than the instrument's length would otherwise suggest. All stopped tubes have this acoustic quality and if that tube is cylindrical (like a clarinet), it misses out alternate harmonics from the list below. If we ignore this irregularity, the set mixture starts off with the fundamental (the note that sounds) followed by an octave and then a fifth above that. Another octave then appears that is followed by a third and a further fifth, with a seventh above that before yet another octave. There are many more harmonics, but at this stage, the first few are enough. To recap, if middle C is the fundamental, your harmonic recipe will consist of C, C', G', C", E", G", Bb" and C"'. These harmonics can be seen clearly when they are played into a frequency-spectrum analyser – you can download one of these from the internet. By experimenting with one and observing the harmonics within each sound, you can deduce that the distinct timbres produced by individual instruments are dependent on the presence or absence of those same sets of harmonics and their relative intensity.

Harmonic Mixtures

Using such a frequency-spectrum analyser, I took 'snapshots' of various musicians' sounds so that I could map out their particular mix of harmonics. I asked some of the players to change the colour of the sound they were producing in order to illustrate what happens when, for instance, they move from a blending and veiled sound to a more penetrating tone. When such colour changes are represented, the sounds will have been performed at the same volume – only a change of timbre will have taken place.

Each graph has a vertical line to represent the intensity of each harmonic and a horizontal line to indicate the pitch. The harmonics within each tone are clearly defined by the peaks in the graph. It is interesting to note that often some of the harmonics appear to be more prominent than the note the ear perceives. Think of the harmonic mixture as ingredients for a cake – you cannot see all the individual components once the cake is baked and if you vary the measurements slightly, the taste alters.

All the instruments were asked to play middle C, and for practical reasons, I have only labelled the pitch of the first ten harmonics in most of the examples. Each player's full spectrum is like an alpine vista: it is far too large and detailed for the book. I have chosen only to show the highest summits to highlight the most striking differences.

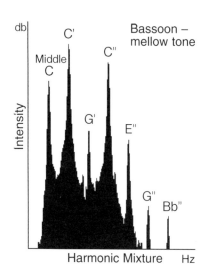

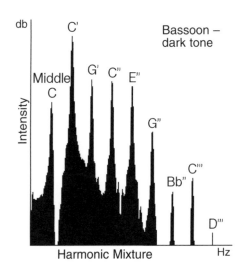

db

C'

Bassoon –
dark tone

Middle
C

G' C" E"

G"

Bb" C'''

D'''

Intensity

Harmonic Mixture

Hz

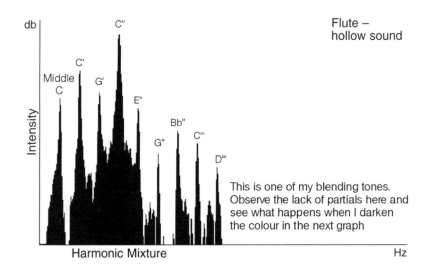

db

C"

Flute –
hollow sound

Middle
C

C'

G'

E"

Bb"

C'''

G"

D'''

Intensity

Harmonic Mixture

Hz

This is one of my blending tones.
Observe the lack of partials here and
see what happens when I darken
the colour in the next graph

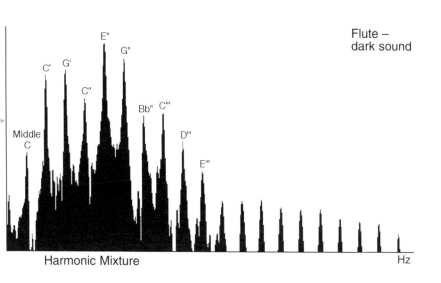

E"

G"

C' G'

C"

Bb" C'''

Middle
C

D'''

E'''

Flute –
dark sound

Harmonic Mixture

Hz

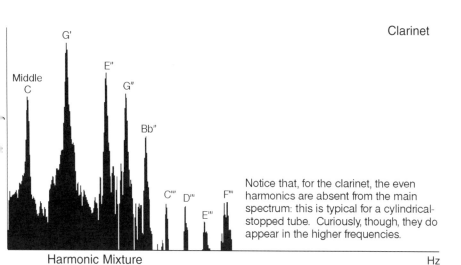

G'

E"

Middle
C

G"

Bb"

C''' D'''

E'''

F'''

Notice that, for the clarinet, the even
harmonics are absent from the main
spectrum: this is typical for a cylindrical-
stopped tube. Curiously, though, they do
appear in the higher frequencies.

Clarinet

Harmonic Mixture

Hz

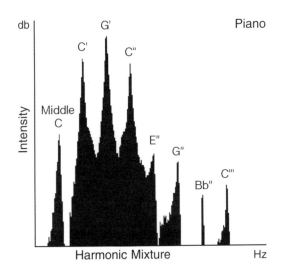

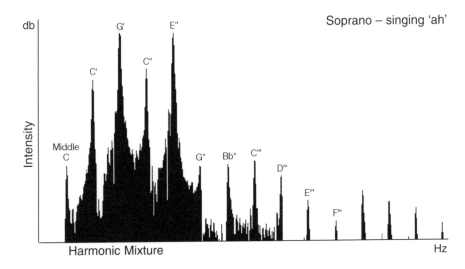

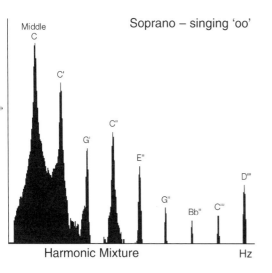

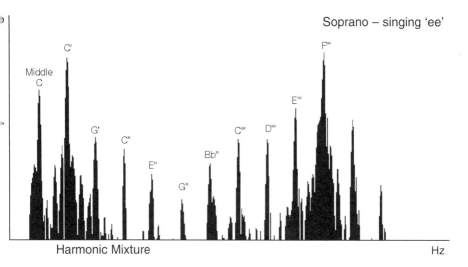

Look at the wide variety of colours which are possible on the violin:

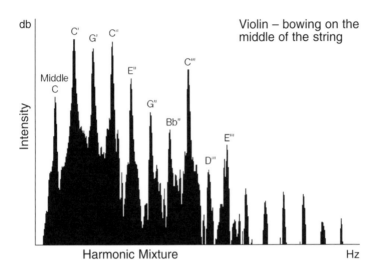

Violin – bowing on the middle of the string

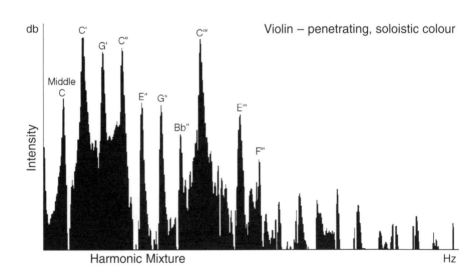

Violin – penetrating, soloistic colour

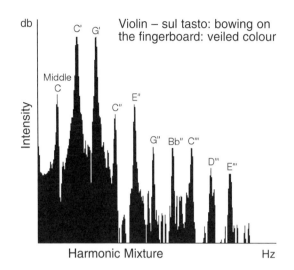

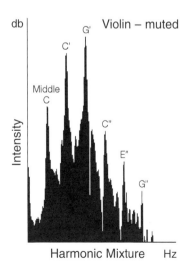

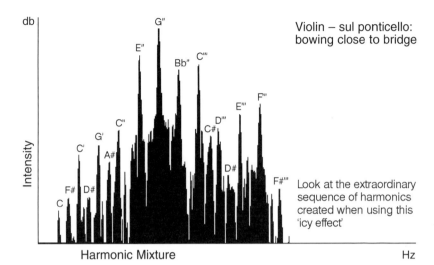

Violin – sul ponticello: bowing close to bridge

Look at the extraordinary sequence of harmonics created when using this 'icy effect'

Harmonic Mixture

The spectrum plots were created, with permission, using 'Spectra-Scope', a type of spectrum-analyser software. For more information, go to *www.spectrascope.com*

• *Experiment with colour changes on your instrument.*
This will add an extra dimension to your playing. It will allow you to blend better with other musicians and create new, amalgamated colours such as that of the 'floboe' and the 'flarinet' rather than those of individual instruments just playing together.

It is through mapping out the intensity of the different harmonics that a synthesizer can impersonate different sounds. It takes a harmonic 'photograph' and then copies it, thus producing a fairly accurate imitation of the instrument in question. Where the synthesizer may fail, though, is with something called the 'starting transient'. This is the 'explosion' of harmonics at the beginning of each note. It is more like a momentary 'fingerprint' of sound in time as it is unique to each instrument, and indeed to each individual player. This phenomenon explains why you can sometimes be deceived about which instrument is playing. For example, if a loud chord masks an instrument's starting transient, you may be momentarily confused between the identities of instruments with similar harmonic structures. For example, those of a horn and bassoon are very similar indeed. However, as soon as the player concerned moves to another note, or, in particular, re-articulates one, your brain will then be able to pick out and label the starting transient, and confirm the identity of their instrument.

Maths Lesson

The first few partials in the harmonic mixture are perfectly in tune with the fundamental and form the basis of our tonality. Although they are not readily audible, they can in fact become quite clear with practice, if you have a sensitive ear. I was taught to hear them by sticking my head inside a piano while my teacher banged out separate notes. At first, you will just hear a ringing sound, but with patience the bell-like quality of the harmonic series should become apparent. One way to prove that harmonics exist is to finger the harmonic series (or part of it) on the piano without actually playing the notes. Hold onto the keys with your right hand so that the respective strings are not dampened, strike the fundamental loudly with your left hand, and then let go. The other notes will ring out in sympathy, some of them sounding louder than others. The octaves should sound as clear as a bell with the sounding fifth (the third note in the sequence) being moderately clear as well; but you may find that the major third struggles, and the seventh will often ignore the experiment. Those two sets of strings will attempt to vibrate in sympathy, hoping to prove that they exist, but they will fail to do so since your piano will not be tuned to the pure harmonic series of the fundamental. We will come to that problem shortly. After repeating this exercise a few times, hit the fundamental again and hold it *without* keeping the other notes down to see if you can identify the heavenly chord within. It is rather like those 'magic-eye' pictures that were all the rage a few years ago. To see the three-dimensional image emerge from the picture, you have to blur your vision to a certain degree. Some people can see the image straight away, while others need training to focus their eyes in a new manner – and many people believe that we are making the whole thing up. The harmonic series within a tone is the same: it has been there since the dawn of time, you merely need to know how to find it. Earlier, I mentioned that the clarinet has some of the harmonics missing from its spectrum. But there are other exceptions to the natural harmonic rule. Percussion instruments like the gong and the cymbal have 'inharmonic' partials that sound – often very loudly – and are unrelated to the note to which they are pitched. Many conductors fall into the trap of accusing the tubular-bell player of hitting the wrong note because an unrelated partial rings out after the fundamental has decayed.

Singing Lesson

We do in fact use harmonics all the time, perhaps subconsciously, taking them into account automatically when we pitch other notes. Singing a third, for example, will consist of your hearing the harmonic series and picking out the third within it. Beautiful though it would no doubt be (assuming that you are not tone-deaf), it would bear little resemblance to the major third on a recently tuned piano. Try it out: play middle C and *sing* an E, making sure the chord sounds gorgeous. Then play the E on the piano. The piano E should sound very sharp, perhaps even painful. You are right, and the piano is wrong. Why? Modern pianos are tuned to *equal temperament* which is based on a particular mathematical calculation, and except in the case of octaves, every note is a compromise.

> 'The modern practice of tuning all organs to equal temperament has been a fearful detriment to their quality of tone. Under the old tuning, an organ made harmonious and attractive music. Now, the harsh thirds give it a cacophonous and repulsive effect.'
> William Pole, 1814–1900, *The Philosophy of Music*, English civil engineer and music scholar

Pythagoras described an octave as the note you get when a string is halved from its original length. In equal temperament, all the intermediate notes between the octaves are produced at exactly equal intervals and not according to Nature's scheme, which our ears are attuned to. Here we have the makings of a dilemma.

Why don't we just tune pianos 'properly' (by the laws of Nature) and leave it at that? Well, if you do get the interval of a fifth, for example, perfectly in tune on the piano (with no beats, as explained later in the chapter) and then carry on tuning upwards or downwards through all the notes in this way, only using fifths and octaves, you will eventually end up getting further and further away from the tuning of your original note. It is like travelling through a labyrinth while someone is moving the walls. If you tune to major thirds instead you will get an even weirder-sounding scale, with the octaves beating wildly. Nature has given us an insoluble puzzle for the fixed keyboard since an octave should not ideally be divided into inflexible parts. Most orchestral instruments can 'temper' their notes to some extent, but a keyboard can't. This has been the biggest frustration for organ-makers over the centuries. While other keyboard instruments' notes decay once hit, the intonation of an organ's note, if not quite right, will stand out like a sore thumb as it continues sounding. I'm sure you will have experienced the 'wowing and beating' sounds of church organs. The most extreme of these were once called 'wolves'.

Making Cents

If you own a tuning-machine, you will have noticed that, along with the pointer that tells you whether or not you are in equal temperament, there are dividing marks that indicate exactly how sharp or flat you are. These divisions are called 'cents' and they are not to be confused with the wave-frequency of the note you are playing. No matter what tuning method you subscribe to, there are always 1200 cents per octave. In equal temperament, this gives us a regular allocation of 100 cents per note. As you progress through this chapter, you will see that in reality they should not be divided equally. Let us return to the tuning of perfect fifths. This interval contains seven consecutive semitones, and in equal temperament that gives us 700 cents in all, but if the fifth is tuned perfectly (see the practical experiment on page 174) the result will in fact be 702 cents. If we tune in a circle of twelve pure fifths, that will give us seven octaves, with the following calculation to make: $12 \times 702 = 8424$ cents. Since I have said that an octave is universally 1200 cents, seven octaves should really equal $7 \times 1200 = 8400$ cents. This 24-cent discrepancy is known as the 'diatonic comma' and trying to eliminate or hide it is called 'tempering'. The big headache over the years has been whether to place the whole of the discrepancy between a couple of notes,

INTONATION

making playing in the related keys unbearable, or to spread it more evenly, so making all the notes slightly out of tune.

As you are beginning to realize, solving the intonation problem is not easy. Many people have come up with solutions, some of them more successful than others. But there is no single intonation scheme that suits all situations. It is a natural instinct for us to rationalize as we attempt to find order in our universe. However, we must not assume that there is always a clear-cut answer. After all, mankind has been innovative and flexible in relation to other problems that Nature has dealt us: our calendar is a good example. We have a natural lunar cycle of twenty-eight days which, after much intellectual bartering (similar to that over the 150 or so temperaments that have been proposed over the centuries), has given us a twelve-month year, each month having a varying number of days. If you look at our chromatic scale, also with twelve notes, you might think of the distance between each pair of them as having a parallel in the lengths of the months which differ, as we have all accepted. Significant distortions that would eventually misalign the seasons are tempered by the leap-year. For minute adjustments, there is also a leap-second that the BBC surreptitiously adds with an extra 'pip' on occasion in the middle of the night. For me, this is similar to the tempering one has to carry out in order to produce chords without beats or wolves. There is actually a society that has proposed that we adopt an 'equal-temperament calendar' with twenty-eight days in each of thirteen months, although their calculations also include leap-years as well.

History Lesson

It was the Chinese who invented equal temperament, thousands of years ago, and although this system was introduced into Europe as early as the 1500s, it wasn't until the 1850s that it became universally adopted. As I have said, many people have experimented with subtle ways of addressing the comma problem. Here are some of the most popular systems, together with their benefits and drawbacks. After each one, I give a table that indicates the movement in cents up or down for each note by comparison with equal temperament, which has 100 cents per interval.

Pythagorean Tuning

This was the basic tuning method that was used up to the fifteenth century. All the fourths and fifths are pure except for the interval between Eb and G# (in this example) which houses the entire comma (24 cents in perfect tuning), and so makes this interval unusable. This system was fine for modal music providing there was no modulation.

C	C#	D	Eb	E	F	F#	G	G#	A	Bb	B	C
o	+14	+4	−6	+8	−2	+12	+2	+16	+6	−4	+10	o

Meantone Tuning

The name Meantone is derived from the fact that the D in this scheme is placed exactly mid-way between C and E: it is the mean. Meantone was used during the Reformation and is based on pure thirds rather than pure fifths, leaving a comma of 22 cents, which is called a 'syntonic comma', to deal with. Although the thirds were delicious, the fourths and fifths were slightly compromised, except for the interval that is usually placed (again) between Eb and G# where a howling 'wolf' appears. Composers sometimes manoeuvred around such wolves by ornamenting excessively. Apart from that problem, this tuning system made basic modulation possible as long as care and thought were given to the keys used. This version of Meantone is Pietro Aron's Quarter Syntonic Comma Meantone (c. 1523):

C	C#	D	Eb	E	F	F#	G	G#	A	Bb	B	C
o	−24	−7	+10	−14	+3	−21	−3	−27	−10	+7	−17	o

There were various attempts to improve and modify the Meantone scale to minimize the wolf and to make the modulations less clumsy. The next big development was Well-Tempered Tuning.

Well-Tempered Tuning

Although Well-Tempered tuning appeared around the same time as Meantone, it wasn't used extensively until the time of Bach and Handel. With this scheme, the comma was spread – albeit unevenly – throughout the whole scale which resulted in the eradication, or at least the taming, of the wolves, producing a chromatic scale that wasn't too uneven and gave great flexibility in modulation. Prior to using a Well-Tempered scale, keyboard players would need to take great care arranging their programmes: works in unrelated keys may have had to appear each side of an interval after a re-tune. The Well-Tempered scale was the one Bach preferred, and to demonstrate its advantages he composed *The Well-Tempered Clavier* in two volumes, both of which contained twenty-four preludes and fugues. The first set was composed in 1722, and the second in 1744. Each set encompassed every possible key, and, using this tuning scheme, they could all be performed continuously.

It seems that musicians of this era did know about the possibility of distributing the comma equally (Equal Temperament), but chose not to do so because they enjoyed the expressive character that each Well-Tempered key possessed. For example, often keys with sharps sounded happy and bright, while the flatter keys would have a dark and sombre quality.

Bach never specified which of the many versions of the Well-Tempered scale he preferred, but it is widely considered to be the case that the following was his choice for performances of his *Well-Tempered Clavier.*

Well-Tempered Tuning (Werckmeister III)

C	C#	D	Eb	E	F	F#	G	G#	A	Bb	B	C
0	−10	−8	−6	−10	−2	−12	−4	−8	−12	−4	−8	0

Equal Temperament Tuning

This is the system your piano-tuner uses. Tuning octaves perfectly, they narrow the fifths (the closest link between Equal and Pythagorean Temperaments) by 2 cents, and so compensate for the augmentation or comma that would otherwise be involved. The advantage with this system is that all the notes in the scale are usable and any modulation is possible. The disadvantage is that all the keys have the same colour, and not one interval is correct apart from the octave.

> 'The fifths are tuned so flat that the ear is not well pleased with them; and the thirds are as sharp as can be endured.'
> Giovanni Maria Lanfranco, 1490–1545,
> Italian theorist

The intonation problems of Equal Temperament were noted back in the sixteenth century, which shows that Equal Temperament wasn't invented to cope with diverse modulations and chromatically complex music but was, on the contrary, ignored until such music made it a necessity.

Let us now look at all these systems together for comparison. This time they are marked in their actual cents value.

	C	C#	D	Eb	E	F	F#	G	G#	A	Bb	B	C
Pythagorean	o	114	204	294	408	498	612	702	816	906	996	1100	1200
Meantone	o	76	193	310	386	503	579	697	773	890	1007	1083	1200
Well-Tempered	o	90	192	294	390	498	588	696	792	888	996	1092	1200
Equal Temperament	o	100	200	300	400	500	600	700	800	900	1000	1100	1200

With this selection of temperaments, you can see the diversity of the solutions that have been proposed over the centuries. However, fine-tuning is still being done, and theorists are still working on the problem. (See Stuart Isacoff's *Temperament*.)

Orchestral Temperament

> Quantz was very much in favour of the sharps being lower than the corresponding flats. I think a lot of modern players may believe they are playing in equal temperament but will be making these natural adjustments subconsciously.
>
> Rachel Brown

There are different types of tempering that are possible when an orchestra is playing. Instruments such as the strings and trombones easily play at any pitch, so that they temper continually. The wind and brass sections (minus the trombones) have mechanical bodies or acoustic means of producing notes that limit the amount of tempering that is feasible. Finally there are those instruments that are fixed such as the tuned percussion: apart from using a saw and some welding equipment, there is nothing the player can do if they are out of tune.

As we assimilate all the knowledge we've acquired in the last few pages, we can now move on to a practical experiment. This will help you to play with a purer intonation. But before continuing, I must offer you a caution as it may change your tuning perception for the rest of your life.

Warning!

Gradually, as your ears begin to hear the natural harmonics described in the 'Maths Lesson' (see page 167), you will start to play with better intonation, as I say. While you continue along this road, you will acquire a highly critical ear, and you will come to realize that no one plays in tune all the time and that pitch rises during every concert. All pianos will make you cringe as you become fully aware of the compromises they require, and you will rarely remain satisfied with your own intonation.

Practical Experiment

The experiment gives us concrete proof of the effects of the fateful comma, and then guides us to meet our enemy, the wolf. We will metamorphose this beating beast into a 'ghost-note'. First, you will need two tuning-machines.
- *It is imperative that you only acquire machines that can 'sing' an array of notes back to you.*
Machines that only listen in equal temperament are, as you will realize, only good for that. They will not help you experience playing in different keys, and they certainly won't give you the flexibility you need to play in tune with other musicians.

When you have gathered together your two tuning-machines,

you should check that they are both set to the same calibration, i.e. A = 440 Hz. Differentiation must be made between the cents we have mentioned and Hertz, as I have said. Cents divide up an octave like the markings on a ruler, and the Hertz number refers to the frequency, or cycles per second, of the note you are playing.

Once they are calibrated, you should set them to sing a major third. You will hear a beat as well as the two notes. The beat fluctuates like a vibrato, but by gradually flattening the upper of the two notes, you can make the beats get *slower*. Flattening it enough will make them stop. When they disappear, the chord will be in tune. Go back to the machine's original rendering of a major third and see what the difference is. The tempered chord should sound rich and transparent like drinking crystal-clear water by comparison to the 'murky' Equal-Temperament version.

Try other chords. You will find that the interval of a minor third will have to be widened, and so on. If you haven't done much sectional work before, you'll be surprised how much 'moving' or 'tempering' has to take place to make chords sound in tune. And so you must:

• *Become flexible with your intonation and learn how to 'move' when necessary.*

Wolves and Ghosts

I am sure you will now be able to appreciate the beats, which fluctuate like a vibrato; but have you ever experienced a ghost-note? If not, get a friend to play some intervals with you: thirds, fourths and fifths work well. Don't use any vibrato, and play as high as you can on your respective instruments. The higher the frequency, the easier the ghost-notes are to hear. Can you hear them? Some notes produce them more clearly than others, and so make changes until they appear. Once your ears develop and learn to focus on ghost-notes, revert to your two tuning-machines again and get them to play some more chords. You may discover that there was an additional note there all along. If you are finding the ghost-notes difficult to locate, ask two flute players to give a demonstration while you stand between them. Or perhaps you might listen to the opening bars from the Finale of Sibelius's First Symphony, op. 39, where there is a 'trio' for two flutes:

followed by a 'trio' for two oboes:

'An interval without combination-tones would
be an abstract concept without being.'
Paul Hindemith, composer, 1895–1963

Once you have a 'ghost-player' present, try tempering the two real notes. The ghost will seem to move in mysterious ways. When the upper of the two notes is moved, the ghost-note follows it, whereas when the lower one is moved, it goes in the opposite direction. This is fully explained in the 'Second Maths Lesson'. To conclude, briefly: if you have a beat, get rid of it; and when you encounter the phenomenon of ghost-notes (or 'difference-tones' as they are scientifically called), you must find a position where all the notes, including the ghost ones, are in tune.

Second Maths Lesson

Middle A has a frequency of 440 Hertz (Hz). This means that the sound-wave vibrates at 440 cycles per second. Playing an octave higher gives us 880 Hz, and an octave lower, 220 Hz, and so on. The average human ear can hear frequencies between 20 Hz and 20,000 Hz (that is, slightly under ten octaves), although some people have been known to hear sounds as high as 40,000 Hz. For tuning accuracy, however, it is widely accepted that we have an accurate pitch-labelling system of around six octaves (60–10,000 Hz).

When two notes sound together, there are two frequencies present. These two wave bands create an additional frequency and if that new frequency is above 90 Hz, our ears will latch onto it. Sometimes we hear it as a beat (the interference between the two sound waves), and sometimes we perceive a note (called a 'difference-tone'). Some theorists assume that beats and difference-tones are 'one and the same', only heard at different rates, while most others now believe that they are distinctly different phenomena. To the performing musician, though, their argument makes no difference as we can use both difference-tones and beats to help our intonation.

The organist W.A. Sorge noted the existence of difference-tones in 1790, remarking that he heard a third deeper note when playing two organ notes together. Organ-makers used this knowledge to bring about the formation of very low notes, for which they would otherwise have had to build extremely large pipes. Instead, such low notes were produced by the difference-tones of two smaller pipes. The pitch of such a note equals the higher frequency minus the lower (the difference).

Here are some examples of chords with their respective difference-tones:

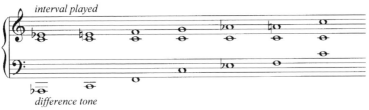

Keuger (1903)

Note that when you get an octave, the difference-tone is equal to the lower note.

The numbers I use in this example illustrate the maths simply: 1000 Hz minus 800 Hz gives a difference tone of 200 Hz.

To complicate matters even more, there is also a 'summation-tone' present (amounting to the sum of the frequencies, and in this case equal to 1800 Hz), although these are very weak notes and only perceptible to a few people. Difference-tones and summation-tones come under the broader label of 'combination-tones' (sometimes referred to as 'subjective tones' as they reside purely within the perception of the listener and do not exist physically).

Let us continue using these figures and see what happens to the difference tone when we temper the chord slightly.

To re-cap, 1000 Hz minus 800 Hz gives us a difference tone of 200 Hz.

Raising the lower note to 801 Hz, we get: 1000 Hz minus 801 Hz, so creating a difference-tone of 199 Hz (the difference-tone goes down slightly).

Flattening the lower note to 799 Hz means: 1000 Hz minus 799 Hz = 201 Hz (the difference-tone goes up). So we can conclude that the lower note and the difference-tone move in opposite directions.

Now let us do the same with the upper note. 1000 Hz minus 800 Hz = 200 Hz; 1001 Hz minus 800 Hz = 201 Hz (the difference-tone also goes up); 999 Hz minus 800 Hz = 199 Hz (it also goes down). With the upper note, the difference-tone moves in the same direction.

Let us now examine what happens when a unison is not quite perfect. Imagine 441 Hz and 440 Hz playing at the same time. The difference-tone would be equal to 1 Hz but we cannot hear that. To the player, however, the result is the same as the interference from these two wave-bands presents a beat of 1 cycle per second.

A near octave of 881 Hz and 440 Hz will deliver a difference-tone of 441 Hz, and yet the listener will not be able to recognize the two lower frequencies as individual notes – they are too close. Once again, the buzz of 1 cycle per second will be heard.

Now that we have taught the tuning-machines to play better in tune, your ear should be improving. How do we apply this knowledge to our playing? As mentioned in the 'Practice' section of the *Nerves* chapter (page 114), a fair amount of improvement can be achieved through osmosis. So undertaking the above experiments will already have improved your perception of intonation. Enjoying the experience of hearing true chords will give you a craving for more; and I find that sorting out just one or two chords in a rehearsal can have an exponential effect as everyone listens more closely, and becomes more attentive and ultra-critical.

When attempting to play in tune with other musicians, we must all be humble, and rid ourselves of the 'I am right and you are wrong' attitude to intonation that has plagued our profession for decades. That means listening, compromising and moving.

The principal oboist of a major European orchestra had, many years before, been a second player in another band. It was his first job, and soon after his appointment he was asked to deputize and play principal in a concert. During the rehearsal he observed that the principal flute-player's intonation didn't match his own. Tentatively, he enquired whether the two of them could try to clean up a few nasty little corners. The answer was surprising: 'No, but don't worry, in time you'll improve.' Not quite the response he was looking for.

It is usually obvious which way you should go if you are the only person playing out of tune. The problem becomes much more complicated and confusing when other people are also at fault. When I entered the profession twenty years ago, mentioning intonation was a *faux pas,* but today there is a much healthier atmosphere, and musicians openly discuss such problems and temper chords in their tea-breaks. Even the most experienced and eminent players know that intonation is like a living being: it is in continual movement at a microscopic level. To play in tune, you have to determine where the intonation is at any point and join forces rather than fighting against it. It may entail adopting the intonation of a previous player or of another section, even if you consider them to be wrong. If someone plays before you, the listener will hear their pitch as correct.

• *When you join another musician on a unison note, only a change of colour should be observed.*

Imagine a transparency lying on top of a transparency, and re-taining clarity throughout. It should be the same with only a change of timbre as different instruments enter. When you play in tune, the picture should always remain clear and in focus, never foggy or blurred.

The Oboe's A

Put this philosophy into practice when tuning up. Many musicians hear the oboe's A but then ignore it as they play their own version loudly. Listen carefully to the sound of the oboe and enter gently. If you can hear yourself rather than just a colour, you are not in tune. When the frequencies are identical, crescendo while attempting to maintain the same pitch. Try it out at home with your 'singing' tuning-machine. This method will increase your sensitivity to pitch as the hair cells on your cochlea become fine-tuned.

Tuning Up Orchestras

The tuning of an orchestra usually takes only a few moments. But under Willem Mengelberg (1871–1951), it could take anything from five minutes to – in extreme cases – two hours.

> 'The first violins are directed to take the A only from the oboe, followed by the seconds, violas, 'celli and basses. The rest of the orchestra then tunes, starting with the flutes and ending with the tuba. Not until the whole orchestra has the A are the stringed instruments allowed to tune their other strings. The oboe officiates like a high priest, and has to stand and turn in the direction of the department concerned, for the benefit of those far away, while Mengelberg, sitting like a Buddha on the rostrum, criticizes the slightest deviation of pitch.'
>
> From *The Orchestra Speaks* by Bernard Shore

The English conductor Henry Wood had a bizarre method of tuning. He would have *two* tuning forks at *different* pitches and go around to every desk and check their intonation. The strings would be calibrated to A = 439 Hz and the wind to A = 435 Hz, making an allowance, he said, for their cold instruments. How long the orchestra played at two pitches each day, I do not know. Later on in his life,

> 'Every member of the orchestra, save the basses and the kitchen department [percussion], were ordered to parade in the artists' room before the concert, not only to ensure that everyone was present but also to take the two As (one wind, one strings) from a home-made barrel-organ which, placed just to the left of the door as one went in, was churned by a rather gloomy-looking man. For half an hour a ceaseless procession of instrumentalists filed past this contraption and tuned their instruments while Wood sat alertly cheerful in his armchair. He would take a good look at each instrument, and say "Too sharp!" or "Too flat" – generally the former. He looked carefully each time because on one occasion a certain string department ("trying it on") brought in the same instrument fourteen times. After that he was wary.'
>
> Again from *The Orchestra Speaks*

Which is Best: Sharp or Flat?

Neither can be the proper answer to this question, although there is a popular saying to the effect that: 'It is better to be sharp than out of tune.' Now, while this is wrong, there is some logic to it. The higher notes on the piano can sound a little flat to the ear: they can sound fine when in chords but perhaps a little 'sour' on their own, for the ear often prefers notes that are a shade sharper than flatter. You may also have noticed that soloists often play sharper – one would hope not too much so – than the orchestra with which they are performing. It eases their projection and creates a brighter sound. To avoid sounding sour, you may find yourself playing a solo at a slightly sharper pitch than you played moments earlier within a chord. But you have to be careful. Pitch rises within every concert, and many instruments have limits to their flexibility.

Accumulating all the knowledge within this chapter should have encouraged you to become more open-minded about intonation. However, are you ready for this? There will be times while you are sustaining a single, long note over a chord modulation when *you* will be the one who has to temper your note to remain in tune!
• *The basic rule is: be flexible and, if it sounds good, it is right.*

Tuning Tips

• *Always sing in your head as you play.*
As long as you can sing in tune, you will pitch to Nature's design. All you will then have to do is continue playing with the same intonation. If you follow other lines as well as your own, you will discover that singing all the time will help your pitching ability. You would be surprised to hear how much better my college students play when they 'vocalize' in their minds. Their intonation, expression and articulation all improve immediately.

If a colleague has a couple of chords that sound out of tune with you:
• *Find a quiet spot and play together.*
Play the notes in question. But first decide who will be doing the

tempering. It will speed things up, since if you both 'move' you may pass each other and lose your way. That is a common occurrence as often the tempering required is minuscule. You might try moving alternately. It will assist the learning process as well as teaching you to compromise. If your tuning doesn't improve immediately, try playing your notes individually so that you can both hear where you are pitching your note. It is sometimes difficult to hear clearly what you are doing when others are playing. If you play on your own, you may find that you were the culprit, which will enable you to sort the whole thing out in seconds.

- *Playing in a good acoustic solves the majority of problems as everyone can hear exactly what they and others are doing.*

Sometimes swapping notes for a moment is a good idea as it will give you someone else's perspective on the tempering involved.

Vibrato is often used as camouflage when there are intonation problems. But it can cause confusion and make the isolation of pitch difficult. Once, when a principal oboe was trying to tune an orchestra using a thick and wayward vibrato, Beecham retorted: 'Gentlemen, take your pick.' It is advisable to:

- *Stop using vibrato when you are tuning.*

You can always add it later, but if you find that the intonation is fine when your vibrato is in the 'off' position and poor when it is 'on', your vibrato will not be compatible. One of you may need to play with a shallower or less intense vibrato. (See 'Vibrato' in the *Ensemble* chapter, on page 91.)

- *If there are beats, you know what to do.*

Listen for beats, and if you can hear them, one of you must begin to move pitch. If the beats speed up as you move in one direction, or as the ghost-note goes even further out of tune, you will be going the wrong way. When the beats stop or the ghost-note is pitched correctly, you will be in tune with each other. Make a mental note of the movement you have deployed and then move on to the next chord. If you feel that you have moved an intolerable distance plead for a compromise and see whether the other player might meet you halfway – something a sensitive player would automatically do anyway. You may find that, once you have tuned a few notes, you won't have to make the same severe adjustments again. If so, you will obviously be playing with acutely sensitive musicians as well as improving yourself. I find a certain amount of sub-conscious adapting goes on each time I try out awkward 'bits'. Sometimes I look in astonishment at a player with whom I have been tuning a chord when we agree that no one now needs to move at all.

Now that I have convinced you of the need to be more flexible with your intonation, you must watch out for the next common fault at this stage. Although you may be playing in tune with a few colleagues after working on intonation for some time, you may have moved away from the pitch of the rest of the ensemble. If that is the case, once you are in tune as a unit, retain the same subtle spacing you have generated and move towards the pitch of the rest of the ensemble.

One often hears a conductor making the mistake of saying to a whole section that is clashing: 'You are all too sharp.' Everyone then plays a little flatter and produces exactly the same clash, only lower.

More enlightened conductors would say: 'Some of you need to be flatter.' However, this doesn't solve the problem of which players this applies to. There is nothing like a mini-sectional in a tea-break – just five minutes will do – to sort out such problems.

- *With chords, always tune from the bass note upwards, and never the other way round: our pitch-labelling system works better that way.*
- *If someone has to play a little sharper to reach you, it may be diplomatic to flatten your note and meet them halfway.*

Still Out of Tune?

If everyone is playing perfectly in tune and you are conscious that placing your note is still difficult, you need to go back to your tuning-machine (the one that sings to you) to re-calibrate your ears. Practising slow scales, or maybe complete solos, with a note singing constantly underneath is very beneficial for your ears and your flexibility, as the placing of any note depends on the key in which you are playing. Identify the note with which you are out of tune, and set the machine to sing at that pitch. In the comfort of your home, you can discover where you are in relation to the player concerned and investigate how you should move to sound in tune. If you feel that a player is sharp or flat in relation to you, re-calibrate your machine accordingly so that you can make that extra adjustment, too.

How Much Work?

Sometimes after you have done a little work on your intonation, everything will suddenly fit into place and become totally clear. But there will be many occasions when the desired outcome will not be achieved. You must aim for improvement in your intonation over the long term and not just for the moment. This is an approach that applies to all aspects of playing.

There is only so much work you can do. After that things will start to get worse through fatigue, physical tension, overcompensation and panic. So:

• *Don't spend too much time on intonation on the day of a concert.*

Eventually your intonation will become better, more compatible and more flexible. You will become familiar with other players' playing, and with which of their notes are sharp and which are flat, and by how much. At the same time – you must never forget this – they will be adjusting to your questionable notes, too.

Chapter 10

The Mechanics of the Orchestra

'Ah music! What a beautiful art!
But what a wretched profession.'
Georges Bizet, 1838–75

In this chapter, I go behind the scenes to look at the daily running of an orchestra. Although there will be slight variations, all full-time orchestras in this country are run in one of two ways.

Self-governing orchestras, which include the four main London orchestras, are run by the players themselves. Some of them are elected to sit on the executive board and possess great power there. Bone-fide members are often required to become share-holders in the company and are paid on a session-by-session basis at individually negotiated rates. Instrumentalists such as the harpist may have a retainer fee included in their contract, as they will not be required for all concerts and they would otherwise have a much reduced income. I once wanted my orchestra to hire someone from a London band for some freelance work. I knew that he was having a week off, but he didn't want to forfeit his retainer fee and so chose not to accept it.

Members of self-governing orchestras may have a minimum percentage of work they have to fulfil each year. Anything above that is voluntary. Many musicians feel obliged to work as in-tensively as they can, and I know of one orchestra that regularly schedules four sessions – two rehearsals and two concerts – on one day.

The accumulation of wealth has not usually been part of the equation for the intellectual and gifted musician.

'I ask not for wages, I only seek room in the garden of song.'
Arthur Wentworth Hamilton Eaton, 1895–1937

Musicians' playing fees can often be so diminutive that they feel they have to play in back-to-back sessions six or seven days a week. This is not a matter of greed but one of necessity, and it is certainly not conducive to the creation of great art. (See 'What Are We Worth?' later in the chapter, page 203.) Another reason for many people having a workaholic mentality is paranoia: if you aren't playing, someone else will be. What if they are better, too? In this business, the fittest survive.

Arduous days can be scheduled in self-governing orchestras because each player can opt out if they wish. Some orchestras may have two principals for each of the sections, allowing the key players to share their hectic schedules between them. Even with such an arrangement, you will find that a large pool of freelance musicians is still required for big repertoire and for times when some of the regular players are not working. You can't have an orchestra with empty seats and missing parts.

I have played in organizations that have a minimum-rehearsal ethic, and allocate at least one day of rehearsals for each programme. Others take on as much work as they can, often sight-reading the music and performing it the same day. It has been known for a single orchestra to accept so much work that they have to appear at different venues simultaneously, which begs the question: which is the real orchestra?

In Britain, there are also *salaried orchestras*. They will have contractual days off and stipulated holidays and will usually provide a pension plan with health benefits.

You may attend concerts played by symphony orchestras with unfamiliar names. They may not be full-time and they may work purely on a freelance basis. You can frequently spot full-time players from well-known orchestras performing in these 'scratch bands' in order to earn some extra money.

The 'tectonic plates' on which orchestras sit are constantly shifting. There is always the threat of axing. Arts Council grants are allocated arbitrarily and they vary greatly between the commercial (i.e. self-governing) orchestras. There are often unsettling rumours of a merger being planned between two orchestras, and occasionally the idea of relocating an orchestra to another part of the country is mooted. When you go to a concert, you will not be aware that there can be an atmosphere of instability within the orchestra of a type which any business in the process of down-sizing would appreciate. All the same, as musicians, we have to go onto the platform and sound like angels.

Behind the Scenes

An orchestra is a complex organism in which many non-players have vital duties to perform. There is the Stage Manager and his team who drive the van to each venue. On concert days, they will arrive up to six hours before the rehearsal begins and leave four hours after the performance. They are trained to move expensive and sensitive instruments around without damage. Often during concerts the stage will need to be re-set for a smaller work, or per-haps a piano will need to be hauled on. The stage-management team will appear at the right moment, dressed in their concert clothes, and carry out the necessary shift.

Recording orchestras also have a Producer and several sound-technicians who will travel to a venue and record an outside broadcast. They will sometimes have to work a fourteen-hour day, setting up the microphones, and balancing and recording the performance. They will later edit the tapes to produce a radio-programme.

All orchestras need people to deal with programming, finance, press and marketing, and they will have a General Manager to oversee the whole organization. On the shop floor, you will find a Music Librarian looking after the orchestra's stock of music, and cleaning, repairing and re-marking parts to make sure the material is uniformly bowed. In the General Office there will be a team of assistants to deal with numerous matters like auditions, fixing, scheduling and recruitment, and they will be headed by the Or-chestral Manager. It is also common for there to be an Education and Community Officer to cope with a variety of projects that in-volve linking up with local schools and music colleges. My re-hearsals are frequently attended by school-children, and members of my orchestra regularly visit schools and perform theatrical/musical stories there.

Our orchestra's non-playing team of administrators consists of seventeen people.

Most of them are musicians or have done music degrees. I think that
helps them understand the players' demands and pressures.

Brian Pidgeon

> 'It is easier to make a businessman out of a musician
> than a musician out of a businessman.'
> Goddard Lieberson, 1911–77
> American recording executive and composer

How Much Does an Orchestra Cost to Run?

Our orchestra costs £5.5 million a year: that works out at about
£15,000 a day. The Bridgewater Hall costs around £5,000 a day, but
then you have to pay the conductor and the soloist, and their fees can
vary tremendously. Depending on the quality of the conductor, his
invoice can range from £1,000 to £20,000 per concert.

Brian Pidgeon
[These figures were for the year 2003–04]

Do Any Orchestras Make a Profit?

No, they try to break even through a combination of ticket sales,
sponsorship, record deals and large subsidies from the Arts Council.
You cannot run a full-time orchestra on ticket sales alone unless you
only do big, extravaganza popular concerts on one rehearsal, with
music that the musicians know well; but the standard of those concerts
is often appalling.

Brian Pidgeon

The funding of orchestras has been so dire in this country that a
bizarre situation arose a few years ago with one group. They were
losing so much money that they decided to cease performing temporarily with the aim of easing their debt crisis.

That was something that crossed my mind as well when I was General
Manager of the Liverpool Philharmonic. At that time, there were real
problems with the city council. It would have been cheaper not to work
as you wouldn't have had to pay out money for soloists and conductors. Before taking my job at the BBC, I went around seventeen
American orchestras. Places like Cleveland and Philadelphia had a staff
of between forty and fifty people just raising money. There is a completely different ethic over there, with members of the public listed
in programmes and on the concert-hall walls, showing how many

millions of dollars they have donated. There isn't that wealth in this country or the tax concessions.

Brian Pidgeon

'Music must be supported by the king and the princes,
for the maintenance of the arts is their duty.'
Martin Luther, 1483–1546,
German priest and scholar

The Duty Sheet

The 'duty sheet' tells the musicians what repertoire they are playing, and what the orchestration, time-table, venue and dress for a concert will be. I am including three examples. There are technical problems when musicians return to play immediately after a holiday, but that is discussed in the next chapter. To make two points at once, the following schedules show each orchestra's first full week back after their winter break.

The first is from the Melbourne Symphony Orchestra (see following page). They receive the whole year's repertoire in November (subject to change) in an impressive, pocket-sized booklet that contains parking information, codes of conduct, dress information and contractual obligations. This innovative publication cleverly doubles up as a diary, with daily entries alongside all the orchestra's requirements. There is enough space for you to be able to write in your social engagements, and your teaching and freelance dates, and so avoid the musician's nightmare of double-booking.

Beneath each piece there are numbers. These are codes which refer to the orchestration, and do so in the following order: woodwind, brass, percussion and then strings. For example: in the Tchaikovsky, the music requires three flautists with the third playing piccolo. Two oboes, two clarinets and two bassoons are also needed to play this piece. In the brass there are parts for four horns, two trumpets, three trombones and a tuba. A timpani player and three percussionists are then indicated before the strings. The numbers that follow in brackets refer to the complement of string players – sixteen first violins, fourteen seconds, twelve violas, ten 'cellos and eight double-basses.

Many orchestras on the Continent and in the USA follow an

**Melbourne
Symphony Orchestra**

			Conductor	Venue	Hours
Mon 28 Jul	Mid Year Break 6				6
Tue 29 Jul	10.00-12.30	Reh Schools	Abbott	355	3
		Meet the Music (performance order)			
	1.30-4.00	Reh Schools	Abbott	355	3
		Meet the Orchestra (performance Order)			
Wed 30 Jul	10.00, 11.15	Schools (years 3-6)	ABBOTT	VAC	3
	1.00 pm	Schools (years 7-10)	ABBOTT	VAC	1
Thu 31 Jul	10.00-12.30	Reh Great Classics 4	Lazarev	VAC	3
	Tchaikovsky				
	1.30-4.00	Reh Great Classics 4	Lazarev	VAC	3
Fri 1 Aug	10.00-12.30	Reh Great Classics 4	Lazarev	VAC	3
	Rachmaninov				
	1.30-4.00	Reh Great Classics 4	Lazarev	VAC	3
Sat 2 Aug	2.00pm	Great Classics 4	LAZAREV		
Sun 3 Aug	Free Day				31
[Mon 4 Aug	8.00pm	Great Classics 4	LAZAREV	VAC	3]

VAC Schools-Meet the Orchestra and Meet the Music.
Repertoire and instrumentation tbc.

JETSET GREAT CLASSICS #4

Conductor: ALEXANDER LAZAREV
Soloist: SIMON TRPČESKI (PIANO)
1   Piano Concerto No 3 in D minor, Op.30   Rachmaninov   39'
        2.2.2.2 4.2.3.1 TIMP 2PERC STRINGS [14.12.10.8.6]

2   Symphony No 4 in F minor, Op.36   Tchaikovsky   44'
        2P.2.2.2 4.2.3.1 TIMP 3PERC STRINGS [16.14.12.10.8]

Notes: 355 is a rehearsal studio
          VAC is the Victorian Arts Centre in Melbourne
          Concerts are notated by having the conductor's name written in capital letters

(Printed with kind permission from the Melbourne Symphony Orchestra)

established pattern of having only one programme per week, which they then repeat a few times. Here is the Oslo Philharmonic's schedule for their first week back after their winter holiday:

OSLO – FILHARMONIEN	GEORGES BIZET *SYMFONISK SUITE FRA CARMEN* *MICHAËLAS ARIE FRA CARMEN*	GIUSEPPE VERDI *OUVERTURE TIL SKJEBNENS MAKT*
DIRIGENT MANFRED HONECK SOLIST ELIZABETH NORBERG- SCHULZ SOPRAN	DIMITRIJ SJOSTAKOVITSJ *MARSJ – POLKA – VALS – DANS* FRANZ SCHMIDT *MELLOMSPILL FRA NOTRE DAME* RICHARD STRAUSS *WIEGENLIED (VUGGESANG)* *ZUEIGNUNG (TILEGNELSE)*	GIACOMO PUCCINI *MIMIS ARIE FRA LA BOHÈME* *O MIO BABBINO CARO,* *FRA GIANNI SCHICCI* JOHANN STRAUSS D.Y. *PERPETUUM MOBILE* *KLÄNGE DER HEIMAT (SANG)* *OUVERTURE TIL SIGØYNERBARONEN*

Sunday 5th January:	free
Monday 6th January:	10-2
Tuesday 7th January:	10-2
Wednesday 8th January:	10-1, and 7.30 concert
Thursday 9th January:	7.30 concert
Friday 10th January:	bus 12pm to Lillehammer
	seating rehearsal, 4.30-5.15,
	concert, 6.30pm
Saturday 11th January:	free

(Printed with kind permission from the Oslo Philharmonic)

For comparison, here is my duty-sheet for the same period:

Week beginning Sunday 5 January 2003 - Week 1 Quarter 1

DATE	VENUE	TIME	EVENT	PROGRAMME/REHEARSAL ORDER	CONDUCTOR/SOLOIST	NOTES	P Hrs	NP Hrs
Sun 5 Jan				FREE DAY (2)				
Mon 6 Jan	Studio 7	1000-1230	Rehearsal	Dvorak / Dukas / Liszt	Jason Lai	Professional Access Scheme strings in today (RNCM students to play in the rehearsal)	5	
		1330-1600	Rehearsal	Liszt / Mussorgsky				
Tue 7 Jan	Studio 7	1500-1700	Rehearsal	Mussorgsky St John's Night on a Bare Mountain 12' 2+p.2.2-4.2+cnt.3.1.-T.-P.-strings; Liszt Mephisto Waltz No 2 12' 2+p.2.2-4.2.3.1.-T.-2P.-H.-strings; Dukas Sorcerer's Apprentice 12' 2+p.2.2+bcl.3+cb.-4.2+cnt.3.0.-T.-4P.-H.-strings; Dvorak The Devil and Kate (extracts) 16' 3(0)+p.2.2+bcl.2+cb.-4.4.3.1.-T.-P.-strings	Jason Lai	PAS strings in today / Pre-recording / Invited audience / Dress: All black	3.5	
		1830-2000	Studio Recording					
Wed 8 Jan	Studio 7	1330-1630	Studio Recording	Sunday Half hour (for BBC Radio 2) Repertoire tbc / Firebird / Vom Himmel	Gordon Stewart / Gianandrea Noseda	Pre-recording	5.5	
		1800-2030	Rehearsal					
Thu 9 Jan	Studio 7	1000-1230	Rehearsal	Firebird / Vom Himmel hoch / Magnificat	Gianandrea Noseda	Meet the Phil 1130-1300	5	
		1330-1600	Rehearsal					
Fri 10 Jan	Studio 7	1030-1300	Studio Recording	Stravinsky The Firebird (complete ballet) 42' 3(p)+p.3+cl/a.3(D/cl)+bcl.-4.3.3.1.-T.-P.-3H.-Pf.-strings Off stage 3tpt 2wdtba+2wdtba; Magnificat / Vom Himmel hoch	Gianandrea Noseda / Lynne Dawson / Mary Plazas / Robin Blaze / John Mark Ainsley / David Wilson-Johnson / BBC Singers	Pre-recording	5.5	
		1430-1730	Rehearsal					
Sat 11 Jan	**Bridgewater Hall**	1500-1730	Rehearsal	in concert order; **Bach (arr. Stravinsky)** Canonic variations on "Vom Himmel hoch" 10' 2.2+d/a.0.2+cbn-0.3.3.0.-H.-10 va + 6 basses - chorus; **Bach** Magnificat in D (BWV 243) 26' 2.2(ob/d/a)+d/a.0.1-0.3.0.0.-T.-cont.-strings; **Stravinsky** Firebird (complete ballet) 42' 3(p)+p.3+cl/a.3(D/cl)+bcl.-4.3.3.1.-T.-P.-3H.-Pf.-strings Off stage 3tpt 2wdtba+2wdtba	Gianandrea Noseda / Lynne Dawson / Mary Plazas / Robin Blaze / John Mark Ainsley / David Wilson-Johnson / BBC Singers	Transmission date 21/01/03 / Pre-recording / Dress: Tails / Long black evening dress / Preview 6.30 / Concert Plus BBC Singers	5	
		1930-2200	Public Concert					

Final travel details will be displayed on the notice board.
Orchestrations and commitments are subject to alteration.

WEEKLY TOTAL HOURS: 29.5 PLAYING HOURS 29.5 NON-PLAYING HOURS 0.0
QUARTERLY TOTAL HOURS: 296.5

(Printed with kind permission from the BBC Philharmonic)

We Don't Work Very Hard!

In my orchestra we regularly have work-experience students sitting in on rehearsals, without their instruments, and observing our daily routine. We frequently hear: 'You don't work very hard, do you?' When you study the actual hours we play together as an orchestra, they may not seem much, but that is only part of the story. We are not paid for the time we spend warming up before each session, nor for the practice we do every night. Many orchestral musicians spend hours inspiring students after work with their teaching, which can be mentally and physically draining. Add this all up, on top of the pressure of performing at the highest level, and you will have a more realistic picture of the time and effort we put into our profession.

Something else that is not accounted for in our pay-packet is the cost of buying and maintaining a musical instrument.

Maintenance

Actors never have to buy their costumes for a play, and secretaries don't have to pay for their new computer or their office supplies. But musicians in this country spend thousands of pounds on their instruments. In some of the wealthier Continental orchestras, the front desk of the strings will be lent superb instruments for the duration of their careers, and orchestras like the Vienna Philharmonic offer such a deal to all their string players. In Britain, nothing like this occurs, although some of the percussion instruments, perhaps a set of Wagner tubas, and the occasional subsidiary instrument like an alto flute, may be provided by the orchestra.

Many players have to possess more than one instrument if they are to survive in the profession because of breakages and the need for maintenance. There is also this problem: when an orchestra is touring in Europe, their instruments usually travel by boat and road. This means that the touring van that carries the larger instruments sometimes has to leave the country a few days before their final concert at home takes place. On such an occasion, half the orchestra may have to play on their second instrument.

Instruments are expensive and they also need maintenance. My flute needs regular body-checks and an overhaul every eighteen months or so, costing around £300.

'Cello Strings

Four decent strings cost over £100. Every string is different, even if they are exactly the same brand. They never sound the same. Some are made well, some are made badly and some strings break. I once got a batch from America. I ordered them on the internet and they seemed a good deal, but one broke every week. My strings always tend to break on the bridge and I look at them before a concert: sometimes you can see the metal lapping starting to uncurl, but usually with me, they just break. There is nothing you can do about it. If it happens in a concert, as principal, I swap instruments with my desk partner who then changes the string for me. She tunes it, and when we arrive at the end of the movement, my 'cello is handed back to me with a new string on it.

Peter Dixon

Oboe Reeds

Outside orchestral rehearsals, I probably spend about eight hours a week making and scraping reeds. I get boxes of bamboo that are grown specially: mine come from the south of France. After soaking them, I gouge the cane, splitting each one into three sections to make one small, thin, straight piece. Then I shape it. It is best to leave a couple of days in between each of these processes to let the cane settle down. The next stage is to tie it onto the staple (the metal and cork device that goes into the oboe) – I use dental floss. It then begins to look like a reed, and I start scraping. From cane to reed takes a couple of weeks but I wouldn't just do one. I would do around thirty at a time. If I'm lucky, fifteen might be usable. This is my personal way of making reeds, but I know other people who can complete the whole process in one day.

Some reeds are good for certain things like low playing, so you pick and choose what reeds you should use for which piece. If one reed is particularly good, you might save it for a special occasion; and so you have to accept that you can't always use your best reed for every re-hearsal. Nightmares do occur: sometimes I will have saved a reed for an important concert only to open my case and find that it has cracked.

Last year, as well as cane, I bought some knives from America, a gouger and some shapers, and it came to £1,200. But now that I have bought the essentials, I expect to pay around £250 per year in the future. Reeds cause us terrible grief and take up a huge amount of time.

We are not credited with these hours. It is the same with practice: we have to do hours at home to stay in shape and we are not paid for that.

Emma Ringrose

Bumping

'Bumping' is employed to save a principal player's lips. It is a daily custom for the principal horn to have a 'bumper' sitting beside him, and the first trumpet may also require one periodically. It is occasionally needed in the wind, too, but more often for doubling purposes to provide a colour change rather than for a lip rest.

> In a way, bumping the first horn part is the hardest job to do, and it is often what young players are given when they first come in. The bumper saves my lip and gives me a rest before a solo. With an inexperienced player, I would bracket what they should play, although in rehearsals I encourage them to play more in order to get a feel for the piece. They need to have a good approach to bumping. If they are a bit kamikaze, then that is unsettling. On the other hand, if they are too timid, they will never get going. It can be a bit daunting if it's your first gig and you don't know what you're supposed to be doing. There is no glory in being a bumper, but if you are an aspiring first horn, it's a great way of getting experience. On the Continent, bumping is less popular. They have a culture there of having up to three principals sharing the work. You have to have a different attitude to playing here because you can't afford to wreck your lips playing flat out tonight if you have a new programme tomorrow.
>
> Jonathan Goodall

Breathing and Bowing

In the wind and brass sections, the players have to breathe! Each principal will indicate where they would prefer the breaks to appear in a phrase, but many advanced players possess the ability to disguise their breaths, and integrate them seamlessly into the music. Some phrases require 'dove-tailing', where the section 'staggers' the breaths, and allows the line to be totally uninterrupted. If you are in doubt about where you should breathe, since there is never 'one right way', just ask. Remember that breathing is 'life' and so you should treat a breath in music, not as an interruption, but as part of the life of the music that lifts the phrase naturally.

With string players, it is crucial that you have identical bow-ings to those of the front desk, unless you have been asked to adopt the free bowing that Stokowski championed. The bows of the strings must be completely synchronized; otherwise, the em-phasis of the string phrasing will be changed, and it will create a touch of comedy for any member of the public who is watching. String players need to keep an eye on the front desk, listen to any orders that are passed back during rehearsals, and observe the markings the players in front add to their music.

> The bowings basically go around on a bush-telegraph system. Desk 2 will have a little look at what I'm doing, and it gradually gets around the section that way. You try and match what you're doing with the first fiddles. Most of our parts are already 'bowed' but the leader may change the odd one, which then will filter through. If we are using brand new parts, the leader will mark up one part, and we all just scribble it in and get as close to it as we can.
>
> Robert Chasey

Transposing Instruments

I remember my grandfather taking me to a concert when I began showing a serious interest in music. He was keen for there to be a classical musician in the family – it was one of his dreams. As a re-sult, he encouraged and educated me for many years, introducing various composers to me, passing on fascinating musical anec-dotes, describing maestros past and present – in fact generally feeding my musical hunger.

The two of us were listening to a performance of Brahms's First Piano Concerto, and I remember being struck by the regal horn solo in the first movement that leapt majestically around. I watched and listened, mesmerized but also confused. The horn solo came back several times in the movement: sometimes it was played by the first horn and sometimes by his colleague sitting two seats to his right. I asked myself: why didn't the principal play all the solos? My grandfather had been teaching me where the various instrumentalists sat in the orchestra, and who would be having the important solos. This didn't seem to fit into his scheme, and he had no solution for me that evening. Over the years I figured it out.

In order to get a definitive answer to my question, we must first look at the history and development of some of today's transposing instruments, and I must thank Jonathan Goodall (horn), Patrick Addinall (trumpet) and John Bradbury (clarinet) for helping me find a path through the transposing marshland.

A transposing instrument is one that transposes the note played to a different pitch. The piccolo is a simple transposing instrument: the player reads a C, and fingers a C, but the instrument sounds an octave higher than written. An alto-flute player would read the C, and finger it in exactly the same way as the piccolo player, but the instrument would transpose the note down a fourth, to sound G – hence its alternative name, flute in G. In both these cases, the composer will have taken this into account. The instrument does the transposing; the musicians concerned think nothing more of it. However, there are musicians in the orchestra who have a tougher time and spend much of their musical life actively transposing.

Around the time of Haydn and Mozart, the horn of the day was called the 'hand horn'. It had no valves, and so the only notes that could be produced in a 'normal fashion' were the ones that appear in the harmonic series (see 'Natural Harmonics' in the *Intonation* chapter, on page 158). It was possible to get additional notes by 'hand-stopping', or closing the bell of the horn with the hand. In scientific terms, this interferes with the 'end-correction' of the tube, and has the effect of shortening it, and thus raising the pitch by a semitone. When this is done, however, the sound becomes very metallic; and even with this timbre change there were still notes missing. In the Mozart horn concertos, there are plenty of notes that would have needed 'hand-stopping' in their day, although there were famous virtuoso players who could produce incredible cantabile sounds that minimized the uneven sonority.

The 'hand horn' had a series of crooks (i.e. bits of tubing) that could change the key and in consequence offered a new set of harmonics from which to choose. The most popular keys for the horn at the time were Eb and D since they tended to produce the nicest sound. Look at all the Mozart horn concertos – number 1 is in D whilst numbers 2, 3 and 4 are in Eb.

It was common practice to divide the horn section of an orchestra in two. The first and second players would probably be pitched in the key of the movement whilst the third and fourth players would be tuned to an allied key: possibly the dominant or the relative minor. If more notes were required than this combination could provide, the players might need to re-crook midway through a work.

Adjusting the length of tubing on a brass instrument is possible as the harmonic series moves in tandem with the change. If, on the other hand, a woodwind instrument could be lengthened or shortened to such a degree, all its holes would end up in the wrong place relative to the tube's length.

The hand horn had various crooks: an A crook, for instance, helped the player pitch the higher notes. But changing crooks took time and so a period of experimentation with valves followed. Finger-operated valves opened and closed different tube-lengths, allowing other sets of harmonics to become available.

> The trouble was: the early valve instruments didn't work very well, and as a result the sound wasn't terribly good. That put off composers such as Brahms, so he continued composing with the hand horn in mind.
>
> Jonathan Goodall

There we have the answer to my childhood question: the solo I had heard was repeated in different keys, and even though the 'valve horn' had already been invented, Brahms still wrote for the older hand horn. The practice of dividing up horn solos between the first and third parts became a tradition and it continued long after the valve horn was universally accepted.

> During the second half of the nineteenth century the valve horn, pitched in F, improved greatly in quality and became widely used. Occasionally a shorter instrument in Bb was needed to facilitate the high register, but the tone quality of these instruments was not generally popular. By 1900, with the increasing demands made by composers such as Richard Strauss and Wagner, a new instrument – the innovative 'double horn' – pitched in F *and* Bb, was developed. Built side by side with a thumb valve to switch between the two different lengths, it gradually became established as the instrument of choice for most players, and is indeed so today.
>
> While we are constantly switching from one instrument to another, we don't actually think of it like that. We just learn the different fingerings for producing the same notes – in a similar way to string players who can produce identically pitched notes by changing strings and shifting their hand position.

As horn-players, we rarely get key signatures (except from Elgar who always seemed to put a couple of flats in). Instead, the composer either wrote in the odd accidental or, more often, wrote 'horn in E' or 'horn in D', etc, midway through the music. This means we have to transpose.

Jonathan Goodall

Question: how many instruments does a trumpet player need to have in order to play in an orchestra? Answer: a lot.

The trumpets I have all make slightly different sounds. One may have more of a soloistic character, whereas another may lie more naturally over a particular shape or phrase. Most of the time in the orchestra I use my Bb or C trumpet, although I own, and occasionally use, the following: rotary trumpets in Bb and C which make a mellower sound – I use them for playing Brahms, Beethoven and Bruckner (some Continental orchestras use this type of instrument all the time). I have trumpets in D, E/Eb and a piccolo Bb. I am about to get a cornet (required for repertoire such as Berlioz), and I also have a bugle for playing on Remembrance Sunday. [This instrument is valve-less, thus relying purely on that all-important harmonic series from which the haunting 'Last Post', etc, is entirely composed.]

Patrick Addinall

How to Transpose

When transposing you must think like this: you go from the key of the instrument you are playing to the key in which the part is written. Imagine reading a D, written in C, which is being played on a trumpet in Bb. Sounds complicated, but just follow the above rule. From instrument to part (Bb trumpet reading a part in C) equals Bb to C. That is, up one tone; therefore, in this situation, everything I read must be put up one tone. I would read the D, and play an E.

Patrick Addinall

The Clarinet Problem

In the intonation chapter, I mentioned that the clarinet was – harmonically – something of an oddity. When a string is halved, one gets the octave above. The same thing happens with the brass: half the length equals double the Hz. An oboe, which is a stopped tube with a conical bore, over-blows the octave, as does a flute even though acoustically they are very different. The flute has an open tube, meaning that air can escape from the top. It also has a parabolic head-joint and cylindrical body but the result is the same as the oboe: it over-blows an octave. In these two cases, octaves are produced either with identical fingerings to those of the lower notes or by using similar fingerings with additional venting. That is not the case with the clarinet. A clarinet is a cylinder with a stopped tube (see page 158), which means that every other harmonic in the regular series is missed out. It over-blows at the twelfth instead of the octave.

> Practically, we have a difficult 'break' as we climb up the scale.
>
> John Bradbury

The other woodwind instruments reach the top of their first register through players lifting their fingers in a logical manner, shortening the tube's length. When they place the fingers back down, perhaps opening a vent or changing the embouchure, the next note in the scale will sound. The clarinet has a few notes' gap before that can be done, and so extra holes have had to be added higher up the tube.

> The clarinet was the 'new kid on the block' by 1700, but its primitive key-work couldn't surmount its unique acoustic property – the gap of a fifth between its registers ('the break'). Instead, early players needed a number of instruments, each pitched in a different key. The instrument has latterly become fully chromatic, but the siblings A, Bb and C remain in the orchestra today. As well as offering the performer an easier ride according to the key of the music, composers enjoy the variety of colours they afford: the longer A clarinet has a darker, mellower sound than the shorter, more pipe-like C clarinet.
>
> As a clarinet player, you have to be able to transpose instantaneously, and if I see students writing out transpositions, alarm bells ring since this ability is needed for a career in the profession.
>
> John Bradbury

The Union

For my first professional gig, I had to join the union. I had no choice and it cost me my entire fee. I had to show my union card to the steward; otherwise the members would have refused to let me play. Nowadays the rules are slacker, and some people join and others don't. There are entire orchestras that 'opt out' and while saving yourself around £200 may seem appealing, it might be short-sighted:

> The Musicians' Union is the second largest organization of musicians in the world, with over 31,000 members, a significant proportion of whom are orchestral musicians. It is the only recognized trade union that works on behalf of musicians in their dealings with employers, whether they be on full-time contracts with an orchestra or a freelance player playing a one-off ad-hoc date. The MU is also influential as a lobbying organization advocating members' causes to the highest levels of government and to many other administrative bodies.
>
> As well as negotiating with employers and setting rates of pay and conditions for just about every type of orchestral concert, the MU offers help and advice in many other areas that touch our professional lives. These include legal assistance, contract and career advice, health and safety representation, benevolent assistance, public liability insurance and many other customized services designed for the self-employed musician. The Union also has a specialist 'section' for freelance orchestral musicians which provides an opportunity for members to express their views and make recommendations to the Union's governing body and via its biennial conference.
>
> Many members think of the Union as an insurance against a whole host of pitfalls such as non-payment and exploitation or sickness, and – speaking personally – the MU has helped me enormously since I began playing professionally in orchestras in the 1980s. It is, in my opinion, a 'must join' organization for all players trying to earn all or part of their living in the UK music business.
>
> Tim Chatterton

www.musiciansunion.org.uk

Rotation in the Ranks

> In our orchestra, we rotate in the strings [which means that, apart from the front desks, the players change their seating position for every programme]. Not all orchestras do this, but I think it is good to play next to different people each week, keeping everything fresh. You would think that sitting at the back would be easier, but in fact having that extra distance between you and the conductor – looking up to find the beat and not having so much contact with the rest of the section – can be quite scary.
>
> Miriam Skinner

Working Your Way Up the Ranks

An orchestra is made up of many musicians all playing their instruments as well as they possibly can: they strive to play in tune and to fit together, some of them blending and others carrying the solos. Some players succeed in attaining principal positions immediately while others never want that sort of pressure and glory. What about those who want to 'move up a notch'?

A few years ago, Julian Gregory moved up within the orchestra, from second to first violin. I remember him telling me there was no extra money involved, and I asked him to explain to me why he had moved and what the difference was.

> Playing the second part is not boring: in fact, it can be quite enlightening to see how a good composer has written the middle part. It gives you a better sense of what is going on harmonically within the whole orchestral arrangement. When you move to the firsts, however, you are playing the lead line and it becomes more satisfying and challenging. You use more of the instrument, so that the technique that you spent years learning at college is being used to the full.
>
> Julian Gregory

Being promoted within an orchestra is often difficult to achieve as you can easily be type-cast. A fresh face may seem more appealing to those concerned than one they know well from within the orchestra. John Bradbury attained his desire of becoming a principal clarinet player when he moved orchestras. But he firmly believes that:

> If you are a good player, you can equip yourself for anything. I was second clarinet in the Chamber Orchestra of Europe for a while, and that was interesting because everyone was paid at the same rate from the Leader right down to the rank and file. Music is a very difficult area when you try to evaluate someone's contribution, and it can all become a bit of a nonsense. Paying each player the same amount made everyone feel that they were valued equally. I played second clarinet in that orchestra as well as I could; but as a second player you may get out of the habit of playing tunes. A back-desk 'cellist, for example, can walk off the platform after a concert having played all of the first subject, all of the second subject and many counter-melodies, too, and having had a rewarding concert. The second clarinettist, however, may not have played any tunes at all and spent the whole concert accompanying and supporting.
>
> John Bradbury

Peter Dixon worked his way right through the Royal Philharmonic 'cello section, starting off at the back as an 'extra'
player. He then got a full-time job as a rank and file member before progressing to their number three slot, although he too had
to change orchestras to make the grade of principal.

> If you leave aside the obvious nerves you experience sitting at the front,
> it's actually much easier playing there: you don't have to look up as the
> beat is right in your face. I found that the real art was playing at the
> back, and I think that learning to play well there stood me in good
> stead for the moment when I moved up. In the job I have now, it helps
> me to understand the problems the rest of the section have regarding
> ensemble, etc. I like to think that I'm always sympathetic, because I've
> done it and I know what it feels like.
>
> Peter Dixon

What Are We Worth?

Players' fees vary from orchestra to orchestra, as I have said. But
let us look at a hypothetical freelancer's earning power in 2004.

Imagine that a violinist is hired to play 'rank and file' in a professional orchestra at the Royal Festival Hall. They are required to
rehearse from 10 a.m. until 1 p.m. There then follows a break
until the evening's concert which starts at 7.30 and is due to finish
around 9.40. How much would you expect that player to earn?
Consider the years of training they will have undertaken to reach
the high standard that is required to play professionally. Think
about the cost of their instrument and its maintenance – all paid
for by the musician – and envisage the personal practice they will
need to do for this particular concert. With all that you have
learnt from this book so far, what price-tag would you put on such
natural talent? Take a guess before reading on.

Whether you have had twenty years' experience or you are
straight out of college, the Musicians' Union 'rank and file' rate of
pay for a three-hour rehearsal plus a concert is as follows:

Category 3: £69.85 – Guilford Philharmonic, Manchester
Camerata, etc.
Category 2: £79.35 – Royal Philharmonic Concert Orchestra,
etc.
Category 1: £92.05 – London Philharmonic, London Symphony
Orchestra, etc.

Chapter 11

Surviving in the Orchestral Profession

> 'To play great music,
> you must keep your eyes on a distant star.'
> Yehudi Menuhin, 1916–99

Once you have auditioned successfully and confronted the many aspects of orchestral playing I have discussed, with good fortune work should come your way. But surviving those initial years in the profession is another serious challenge. I hope that when you read this chapter, you will find in it some survival strategies which will increase your confidence and your knowledge of what is involved.

Being Booked

You have proved yourself as a musician either through auditioning or by word of mouth. Your name will now be passed on to the orchestral office and added to a list. If you are selected for a trial, the fixer will phone and offer you some work. If, however, you have just been put on the extra-work list (see the *Auditions* chapter), this will not necessarily be a guarantee of future work. Some principals only put musicians on their lists they intend to use, while others seem to include every player in the offing. Few of them would consider using players from the bottom of their pile. Ergo, if you are on a list but no work is coming your way, it might be worth your while re-auditioning. Your hope would be to step up a couple of rungs. But there is a danger. Orchestral lists can function like a 'snakes and ladders' board: many players may be moved down while attempting to climb higher.

The Fixer

If you do get booked for some work, the person who rings you will be called the 'fixer'. The fixer will be your bridge to the orchestra and their role is often underestimated.

> One of my duties is to be the fixer of the orchestra: if anyone goes sick, they phone me and I find a replacement. When we are doing large works, I look at the orchestration and book all the extra players who are required. I make sure that all the jigsaw pieces fall into place, with everyone sitting in the right place at the right time – hopefully with their instrument. This last point may seem obvious, but I booked a bassoonist once who turned up for a 10 o'clock rehearsal, saw that everyone was ready to play and asked: 'Oh, do I need my instrument?'
>
> I get to know who the principals of each section favour, and which players to book. With the strings in this orchestra, there is a definite hierarchy: I know exactly who to phone, and in what order. With the wind and brass, it is a little more complicated. They still have an order to their list, but as the freelancers coming in will be playing separate parts, I have to check with the section principals each time because every player has individual strengths that may be required for the repertoire being performed.
>
> Occasionally, when there is an emergency, we find it difficult to get someone at short notice. This is a problem that is easier to cope with in the strings as so many of them play the same part. You can get away with being 'one violin down', but there would be holes in the music if wind or brass players were not replaced.
>
> Recently, the contra-bassoonist phoned in sick at 8.00 a.m. and the pressure was on. There was a commercial recording starting at 10.00, and there aren't that many contra-bassoonists living in or around Manchester. It was very stressful, but we found one at 9.30. It is a challenge when these things happen, and I really enjoy the relief once things have been sorted out.
>
> Helena Miles

A Fixer's Top Tips

- *Carry your diary with you at all times.*
- *Always phone the fixer back, even if you can't do the work.*
- *If you hear your phone ringing at 8 a.m. it is probably a fixer, so answer it!*
- *Keep the orchestra office informed about any telephone-number changes, and let them know if you move house.*

It is so important to have your diary with you. If you don't, then you must ring the office back as soon as you can when you have a message from them. When you are a fixer and you are going through a long list of players and making endless phone calls, it is frustrating when the people you're talking to can't give you an answer straight away. My job is so reactive. I have to wait for them to respond, and it is always the same people who don't have their diary with them. I know what they are going to say, and I just have to wait for them to call back. Often they don't. If you are a musician looking for work, please buy a small pocket diary and carry it with you at all times.

Helena Miles

• *Never double-book yourself.*

It is really annoying for all of us when people double-book themselves. This happens particularly with students. I once had someone working with us as a freelancer, and he came into the office the day before one of our concerts saying that he would have to miss our dress-rehearsal. He had only just realized that he was due to play in a lunch-time concert with his college chamber orchestra at the same time. Often students just say 'yes' without checking their diary because it is professional work they are being asked to do. But when things like this happen, I have to explain the position to the section leader who would think twice about booking that player again.

Helena Miles

I rang to tell a fixer that I had double-booked myself. She slammed the phone down and I was never asked to play with that orchestra again.

Brian Pidgeon

As fate would have it, Brian later became General Manager of the orchestra concerned.

• *Always be polite to the fixer.*

The fixer is your link to the profession. If you are 'off-hand', or if your attitude is wrong, that can also put a black mark against your name. We had a situation where we had begun a recording session, but because of a duty-sheet mix up, two freelance wind players were missing. I phoned the first of them, who was so apologetic. She couldn't believe that she was late, and rushed to our studio as fast as possible. Whereas the other player's response was: 'I can't possibly come now. I'm shopping.' I had to explain that the whole orchestra was waiting for her; the commercial recording company was all set up and ready to record; and we couldn't start without her because she had a solo part. What's even more unbelievable was that she was on trial. We were all in a state of shock after that response.

Helena Miles

- *It is important to check what instrument and what position they expect you to play.*

This is particularly important if the orchestra doesn't know you very well since mistakes can happen. There was once a fixer who needed to get a leader for some work, and wasn't having much luck. In desperation she rang another fixer for names, and at the same time asked for 'cello players as well. She was given a long list. She started at the top and worked her way through. No one was available until she got towards the bottom. The player she hired didn't say what instrument he played, and she was so happy at having solved the problem, she didn't check either. Fortunately, the error was spotted the night before but, for a while, a 'cellist had been booked to lead an orchestra!

Helena Miles

- *Check that you have all the correct details.*

One of the perks of my job is ringing up people and giving them their first stab at professional work. However, they are often so thrilled that they miss important details; and so if anything is unclear to you when your phone call is over, just ring back and be honest. You were excited.

Helena Miles

The Route to Work

In this section, I follow a successful music student's trail from graduating right through to being offered a job in a full-time orchestra. I knew Emma Ringrose when she was studying at the Royal Northern College of Music and interviewed her exactly one year after she became our second oboist.

When I left music college seven years ago, I wrote to all the orchestras in the region asking for extra-work auditions. I should have done it earlier because I didn't realize that the process can take quite a while. It may be a year before you are heard by some orchestras, and with others you don't get a reply at all. It depends on how efficient the people in the office are as well as on how many players they already have on their list. My teacher at college was the Principal Oboist with the Royal Liverpool Philharmonic, and they gave me an audition straight away. I think everyone goes through a period of panic when they suddenly become aware of how high the required standard is to play in the profession. There was certainly a time when I thought I wouldn't get any work, and so when the 'Liverpool' rang, offering me a gig one month after leaving college, I was thrilled.

I went to the first rehearsal and remember not being able to speak to anyone. I didn't know what to say because I was so nervous. Luckily, I was doubling the second part in Beethoven's Ninth Symphony, which was a nice introduction to the profession. [Doubling is occasionally used in the wind section for two reasons. Having two players on each part creates a wider timbre when they double up for some of the louder passages; but the extra players can also be used for 'bumping' – described in the *Mechanics of the Orchestra* chapter.] The biggest shock was how quickly they worked because they all knew the piece backwards.

After that first concert, the phone calls were few and far between. There were many players above me on the list, and I knew that it would take time to work my way up the ranks.

To supplement my income, I taught. I went to the library and found a book with all the schools in the area, and I wrote to a lot of them asking for teaching. It wasn't the best standard of work, but it was quite easy to get – although I had to tutor all the woodwind instruments. At college, I had attended 'art of teaching' classes that turned out to be very useful as the fundamentals of all the wind instruments were taught. However, doing so much peripatetic work, I was worried that my playing standard might slip. To make sure that my lip was always in shape, I usually practised for an hour and a half when I got home from my teaching. Gradually, I think my name was passed around because work with other orchestras (whom I hadn't auditioned for) began to trickle in.

One thing that I wasn't expecting was that I needed to have slightly different reeds for every orchestra I played with. Each band expects you to play in a different (or a distinct) way. For example, an opera orchestra I used to freelance with played quieter than I had expected, and so whenever I was going to play with them, I tried to make a reed that had *pianissimo* qualities. Another orchestra played at a slightly higher pitch and so I had to make shorter reeds for when I was playing with them. [Emma discussed reed-making further in the *Mechanics of the Orchestra* chapter, on page 194.]

A group that I got involved with for a while was 'Performing Arts'. They perform every weekend throughout the summer which is useful for freelancers as there isn't an awful lot of work going around at that time of year. Everyone in fact is hired on a freelance basis, and you all feel on an even footing. The concerts are performed outside and they have a lorry that turns into a stage. The audience picnics in a field and listens to the music there, often in the rain. We did a lot of different programmes, so that it was never boring – but it could be painful! It was often cold, the programmes were long, and you knew that you would leave the platform with your lip hanging off. Outside, you do tend to play louder than in a concert hall, and I don't think that it is necessarily good for your playing. On the Performing Arts stage, there are microphones that are constantly on, so you can't warm up or practise too much because they could hear you within a three-mile radius. The hours are crazy, too, as you could quite easily be on a coach from 10 o'clock in the morning, travel for about seven hours, get to the field, rehearse and then (after a break) have to play the concert. With all these things, it is easy to get out of the habit of warming up, and that is a great danger.

When I auditioned for my job, I was quite pleased with how it went. I was better prepared musically and mentally than in any other audition I had done. I was given a trial and, over a year, played with the orchestra for seven or eight weeks before I was offered the position.

As the second oboe player, I have to be able to match the first. I need to blend with their style, their intonation and articulation. I also must be ready to step up at a moment's notice: I'm like an understudy. Playing in an orchestra has lived up to my expectations, although I was warned that the first year would be hard, and it was. An orchestra is like a family, and when you join, it can be difficult to know where you fit in as everyone already has their own clique.

The amount of repertoire is immense; everybody else knows it; and there isn't a lot of rehearsal time. Everything is recorded in this band so that it is difficult to maintain the standard that I want to play at, and I have never had to make so many reeds in my life. There have been times when I have wondered if I could cope.

Emma Ringrose

All Those Notes to Learn

I too felt buried under the sheer quantity of music our orchestra got through when I first started working. I was aware that eventually I would learn most of the repertoire, but that didn't solve my immediate problem which was that of learning the notes quickly for each evening's concert. Three pieces that I distinctly remember not being able to get anywhere near were, Strauss's *Don Juan*, Stravinsky's *Firebird* and the last movement of Rachmaninov's Second Symphony. They were all pieces for my first tour, and they were far more difficult technically than anything I had previously played. I had to think logically and rapidly, and I decided to prioritize. I worked on the exposed bits first before attempting to sort out the rest. With our work load, it would not have been possible for me to have learnt all the notes for every concert, and so each time I played those pieces, I made sure that I got a little bit closer. I knew which passages I couldn't quite manage, so I hid or 'ghost-played' those bits and then sang out in the solos. The secret is to know what you can and what you cannot do. It is normal for young professionals to find that it can take them several performances before they feel secure, although I did feel extremely guilty at the time – thinking that orchestral musicians always played all the notes.

> We played Mahler's Fifth Symphony recently. It was the fourth time I had played it, but it was the first time that I had felt comfortable and actually started interpreting the music. So often, with the amount of notes we have to learn, playing in an orchestra can become very black and white: you just stick your bow in the right direction and finger the right notes, and that's all. That can have a knock-on effect on your playing.
>
> Miriam Skinner

Networking and Common Mistakes

> I don't think that getting work in the first place is necessarily as hard as being asked back. Sometimes, as a freelancer, you feel you're being judged all the time, and you can seem like an outsider. I was always careful to do what I thought was expected from me as an extra player. I bought the teas, I complimented players and I never laughed when somebody made a mistake. I never drank alcohol before a concert, and I didn't cross my legs. I think it looks sloppy and suggests you don't really care. I also didn't scrape reeds in rehearsals, even though I do that now as a full-time member. Maybe that is unfair, but it was one of the rules I had for myself: it can be noisy and off-putting, and it can be easy to miss your entries, if you're making reeds.
>
> Emma Ringrose

Whether you like it or not, you *are* judged as soon as you enter the rehearsal room. Your playing will be put under the microscope and your personality will be scrutinized as well. If the members of the orchestra can't get on with you, then they won't be able to work together with you. Information about you will be passed around and may influence how much work you get with that orchestra in the future.

If you are a wind or brass player, your playing will be easy to assess since you will be sitting near the principal of your instrument; but, string players, unless they are on trial for a 'numbered' post, will probably be sitting at the back where they:

> Could be knitting or growing vegetables, and one would not know.
>
> Robert Chasey

When new string players come in to play with an orchestra, they are often asked to sit in different positions so that they can be assessed by players who are closer to the front desk.

> I try to make sure that everyone in the section sits next to trialists so I can get feedback. Obviously what matters is that the rest of the section gets on with them personally as well as musically. If there were two equal players, I would give the job to the one the section preferred. It is such a pressurized situation that we are in as performers, and any extra tension is going to be detrimental to the way the whole section performs.
>
> Peter Dixon

In an office, you can close the door to get a moment to yourself. In an orchestra you are together as a unit, in the same room, all the time. Every player is interdependent, and it is crucial for the musical standard and for the smooth running of the orchestra that personalities don't clash. However, sometimes freelancers can try too hard:

> The thing that I really cannot abide is people who are obsequious. They push to the front of the coffee queue to buy you a cup; they try to ram their CV down your throat; and every time you play a note, they come up and say: 'That was absolutely marvellous.' When I was younger, I was painfully aware that some of my colleagues, who were going for jobs, were 'grassing up' to the principals: it was nauseating. Another mistake that some players make is to come into rehearsals before the session starts, and show off. Playing your concerto repertoire very loudly upsets people, and is totally misguided. [See 'Back-Desk Soloists' in the *Ensemble* chapter (page 110).] In an orchestra, few players behave like that because most musicians enjoy being part of a team.
>
> Peter Dixon

Getting the balance of networking right is therefore tricky. I asked freelancer Nic Dowton to tell me what her approach would be.

> Unless I know a player well, I only speak when I'm spoken to. A lot of musicians live in their own world, and they don't necessarily want a freelancer who chats incessantly. They may just want you to sit there and play.
>
> In rehearsals, I sometimes see people doing things wrong and know that they are jeopardizing their future. It depends what position you are in. For example, if you are playing 'down the line', you should never play so loudly that you are asked to 'be quiet'. It is better to be asked for more support rather than being told to 'shut up', as that would mean that you have not been sensitive to what has been going on around you.
>
> Pitch is vital and yet, so often, people who are insensitive to tuning continue to blast out their bad intonation. I notice people playing notes longer and louder than their colleagues and have observed vibrato, breathing and rhythmical discrepancies between players – and all these things are mistakes.
>
> The more work you do, the more confidence you will get. But I find that at every single rehearsal I'm still learning, and I like to think I'm still improving. If you think that the standard you leave college at is good enough for the rest of your career, then the harsh reality will be that you're just not working hard enough. You should be able to improve every week.
>
> Nic Dowton

After every concert, analyse how you could improve. Consider how to make progress in all the basic techniques, and how to develop ways of fitting into your particular section with greater ease. Evaluating your playing positively should enhance your next performance.

> I think having that sort of attitude keeps one's playing fresh and maintains a standard that is going to match that of the students leaving college. They may have been doing many hours of practice every day and, if you're working, you don't have that luxury. You need to improve continually in order to keep up with everybody, and you must realize that you can always be replaced. There is always the threat of a star player suddenly appearing on the scene who is better than you. And so, with a freelance career, there can never be any guarantees.
>
> Nic Dowton

Keeping in Shape

Although you may now be playing professionally on a regular basis, I'm afraid that that will still not be the end of the story. Continuing to practise is crucial. Even if perfection in music is unattainable, the quest for it should be unrelenting.

Most performers will have practice routines to enable them to stay in shape. These will not involve practising repertoire for particular concerts but exercises for producing sound that stretch and flex the appropriate muscles. Personal warm-up patterns help maintain consistency and improve one's fundamental standard on a daily basis. My set routine has hardly changed in twenty-five years, and yet it continues to keep me in shape.

> When playing any musical instrument, the difference between right and wrong, or good and bad, is such a fine one that the control level required goes beyond most people's imagination. If you consider a top athlete like the tennis-player André Agassi, he doesn't just take his racket out and hit tennis balls around each day: he has to do exercises and routines to improve his whole game. He trains hard in the gym to maintain his fitness, increase his stamina and achieve a balance in his muscular structure – so that the stresses and extremes of the tennis match are not beyond his physical capabilities. Playing a musical instrument doesn't require such athleticism, but far too often people see playing a musical instrument purely as an academic exercise. That may be part of the picture, but what is not recognized is the physical discipline that is required if players are going to maintain a standard. The comparison between athletes and musicians is no longer meaningful when it comes to the pressure involved in being accurate. If the striking of a tennis ball or a football is out by a *centimetre* on contact, then it may not be the best shot in the world, but you would still be 'in the game'. On the other hand, if I were to hit a note one *millimetre* out of place with my lips, the correct note would probably be over an octave away – the equivalent of hitting the ball into another court. The warm-up routines I did for about seven or eight years made an enormous difference to my playing, and took around an hour and a half. That is, purely exercises and no repertoire: the equivalent of stretching in the gym. Now, the routines I do are more specific to my needs and the time spent each day varies according to requirements and aims.
>
> Patrick Addinall

There is an exercise book for flute players entitled *How I Kept in Shape*, which was written by Marcel Moyse (1889–1984). Over the years, this internationally acclaimed teacher and soloist, who was principal flute of the Opéra Comique in Paris, collected and stuck into a scrap-book passages from the repertoire that encapsulated what was important (and difficult) for him on his instrument: a cadenza from an orchestral work, an articulation study, a slow vocal line from an opera, etc. He did this so that he could take all his favourite 'tricky' musical passages with him, and keep in shape without carrying hoards of books, whenever he travelled. I tell my students to look at this book and then make a compilation of their own. Their versions may contain similar passages that reflect aspects of playing which are universally difficult, but they will also include quite different material that is precisely relevant to their needs. What one person finds easy, another may find demanding.

Waiting in the Green Room

Extra wind, brass and percussion players will be booked for entire sessions even though they may only be required to play for ten or fifteen minutes in a piece. They may spend more time chatting to other extras in the green room than participating in the rehearsal. Waiting for the conductor to come to 'your' movement may seem like easy money; but hanging around for extended periods of time can have a destructive affect on your playing. Extra players mention this as a problem as they anxiously rush on to play, when it is suddenly their time, and desperately try to get into the right frame of mind. Percussionists are often in this position as many pieces have little for them to do. In my orchestra, the percussion section is positioned so that they have easy access to an exit. There is an adjacent practice room with instruments set up for them, and they can wander in and out without disturbing the flow of the rehearsal. With intuitive timing after years of experience, they saunter back at exactly the appropriate moment. In an attempt to counteract the tedium of sitting around as they wait to play each day, one of our percussionists told me that he works through a variety of techniques he learnt at college to maintain his playing skills. He practises every day at home for about an hour and has percussion equipment permanently set up in his house – for if it wasn't, the temptation would be not to bother at all.

Tours

Going on tour with an orchestra is not a holiday. But it can be great fun. The average orchestral tour is so hectic, with arduous travel schedules and mounds of repertoire, that all you usually see is airport lounges, concert halls and a few bars. Keeping your playing in shape on tour is tough since often your instrument will be travelling on the orchestral van and if you can 'hand-carry' it, you then have the quandary of whether to play in your hotel room. Once, when I was touring in Japan, I got an irate long-haul pilot banging on my room and demanding me to stop practising. If your warming-up pattern may have to be adjusted, the pros of touring do outweigh the cons. Although you don't have the chance to see much of the countries you visit, you will still get the flavour of many different cultures, which will enrich your mind. Performing concerts daily helps you to keep in shape; the bonding between players on tour is invaluable for keeping the morale of the orchestra high; and you will stay in hotels you could never otherwise afford.

Holidays

There is an old proverb. Take one day off and you will notice. Take two days off and your teacher will notice. With three days off, the audience will notice. It rings true. So how do musicians cope with holidays? It is impossible for us to go on a two-week vacation and then return to play at the same standard. For example, the lip muscles of a flautist and the stamina and suppleness of his fingers will begin to seize up the moment he stops playing. Considering whether to put your instrument into hibernation for a few weeks can face you with a real dilemma. Most people in general try to forget about their work when on holiday, but if we didn't have a structured timetable leading up to the end of our break, we would face embarrassment on our return. Orchestral players have to perform at the highest standard straight away. There are no slow days after a holiday; there is no easing back into a tough schedule; there are concerts and recordings immediately. The audience won't be too happy to be confronted with a 'first day back' ensemble. When I spoke to a principal wind player in the Royal Philharmonic many years ago, she told me that it always took her three weeks to get fully back into form, and feel really comfortable with her playing.

I have tried several methods of combating this holiday problem. I firmly believe that playing for a couple of hours each day is obligatory if you are to maintain your standard; but doing that will ruin your well-deserved break. Playing for only a modest time every day will still ruin your holiday and it will achieve next to nothing. Not practising at all until the penultimate day, on the other hand, will be utterly disastrous as you painfully force your muscles back into shape. The usual solution is to build up gradually towards the end of the holiday. This means either taking your instrument along and picking it up towards the end, or returning home early and cutting your holiday short.

> If we have a long enough holiday, then I do take some time off playing because I think that, quite apart from having a rest, it is a good idea to start from basics every now and again: you can scrutinise the foundations of your playing afresh. If I have a three-week holiday, the last week will be spent practising and getting my playing back into form. I notice that I need to do slightly less practice each year to reach my standard. But the time will never come when I can just take my trumpet out of its case and play at the same level I was at before a holiday.
>
> Patrick Addinall

Survival Tips

• *Arrive on time.*
It goes without saying that you should arrive at rehearsals in good time to prepare yourself and feel comfortable. You shouldn't come in late and red-faced, weaving in and out of ninety musicians, and nodding apologetically to the conductor, while receiving heckles from the brass section.

Many orchestras throughout the world have morning rehearsals (with the afternoon off) on the days of concerts, and some time ago a London flute player used this opportunity to go back home, taking her music with her. She was caught in flash-floods and couldn't get to the concert on time. It was a Prom, and live on the radio. The concert was to start with Mendelssohn's *A Midsummer*

Night's Dream overture, which begins with lone chords on two solo flutes: there was nothing they could do except wait.

• *Always be cheerful ...*

> No one wants to work with someone who is miserable, especially if they are a freelancer: they just wouldn't want to sit next to you if you were moody.
>
> Nic Dowton

In an orchestra, nobody wants to see a sour face, even if you made a mistake during the last session.

• *... and gracious*

When complimented, try to be gracious no matter how upset you may feel about your playing. Many musicians fall into the trap of listing their faults as soon as a flattering remark heads their way.

> Try and be humble, but don't try too hard, and never brag about other work you are doing.
>
> Ben Hudson

In every orchestra you will find cliques of players huddled together. Don't be offended if they ignore you. It is nothing personal. They are probably talking about some political problem within the band, and, believe me, there are loads of those.

> Veer away from talking about orchestral politics if you are a freelancer. You can listen, but voicing an opinion may come back to haunt you.
>
> Nic Dowton

• *Take a pencil to all rehearsals.*
• *Check that you have the music and your instrument with you.* There are many stories about musicians picking up surprisingly light instrument cases, only to find them empty when they get to a rehearsal.
• *Have your diary with you at all times.*

Many musicians, especially freelancers, join a diary service. Such organizations hold your work information and know which days you wish to remain free. They act as an intermediary, letting fixers know whether you may be able to accept work. The cost (at the time of publication) is around £540 (including VAT) per year, but it won't guarantee employment. That is up to you and your reputation.

• *Don't look over at someone's part when they are playing.*

This can become a habit, and it is amazing how off-putting it can be. In a similar vein:

• *Resist the temptation to turn around and look at a musician who is playing a solo.*

'Lighthouses', as we like to call them, won't win in a popularity contest. And:

• *Only play other people's solos in the privacy of your home.*
• *Cut out the choreography!*

As compared to our Continental counterparts, musicians in British orchestras don't move around much whilst performing. Many freelancers are 'scrubbed' off the extra-work list for excessive 'manoeuvring' and for leading from 'down the line'. You don't need to be rigid, but you might put off your desk-partner by physically bringing in the whole section – unless, of course, that is your job.

• *Deodorants, cologne, perfume and photos.*

That you should pay attention to your personal hygiene is obvious, but you should also take into account the fact that some people have an allergic reaction to perfume. Think of poor wind and brass players breathing deeply before their solos and having a seizure as a result of your abundant and potent cologne.

Occasionally, you may find photographs and amusing quotes placed in your music. Once, in the middle of a concert, I turned a page to find that the next section of the music appeared upside down and in the wrong order. If you don't like surprises, check your part thoroughly before you play. It may spoil someone's practical joke, but it could save you from embarrassment.

• *Buy the teas.*

> It is just good manners: they've given you the work, and so buy them a cup of tea in the break.

Nic Dowton

Chapter 12

Alternative Careers

'Without music, life would be an error.'
Friedrich Nietzsche, 1844–1900,
German classical scholar, philosopher and critic of culture

This book is primarily intended to help orchestral instrumentalists succeed in playing with a modern symphonic orchestra. What happens, though, if you train yourself towards achieving that goal and then decide that orchestral playing is not quite the thing for you, or that you want to add variety to your musical life? There are countless alternatives, and it would be impossible to list all the permutations there might be. All the same, I would like to throw some ideas into the ring while remaining close to the core concerns of the book. I had interviews with five very different musicians which I present to you as case studies in the hope that they will give you inspiration. All five musicians steered totally different courses from each other, although the orchestra continued to be important for them.

Chamber Music

Many symphonic musicians would actually prefer to be playing chamber music rather than the orchestral repertoire. The music is more intimate and rehearsals can be less pressured and more democratic. I spoke to the violist Roger Bigley who has had several shifts in his career. He was a founder member of the Lindsay String Quartet, playing with them for over eighteen years. He moved to my orchestra as co-principal viola, and is now second in command of the string department at the Royal Northern College of Music. I asked him about his background, and about the different qualities that are needed for playing in a chamber ensemble as opposed to a large symphony orchestra, and then to describe his move into administration.

The majority of string players at music college have the desire to be a soloist or a chamber musician. That is their goal, and becoming an orchestral musician is not usually so high on their priority list. Stringed instruments are capable of a greater emotional expression than some other instruments, and that is why composers have written some of their best and most expressive repertoire for the string quartet. The ease with which strings can be flexible with pitch, and the intense rehearsal required for string chamber music, leads to very expressive harmonies and a greater depth of ensemble understanding.

The Lindsay String Quartet began its life when we were students studying together at the Royal Academy of Music. We won several prizes, and towards the end of our college career we responded to an advertisement for a young string quartet to be resident at Keele University. This scheme was the brainchild of Professor George Pratt; it was funded by the Leverhulme Foundation, and it involved the Russian violinist Alexander Moskovsky, who used to be in the celebrated Hungarian String Quartet. One player in our quartet was not interested in the scheme, preferring to stay in London rather than move to the Midlands, and so, after a change of personnel, we went for the job, and we got it. The residency entailed giving concerts, teaching within the faculty and joining in with the university's symphony orchestra. The music department itself was small but there were many keen musicians studying other subjects. During the five years we were at Keele, we were able to devote hours to personal and ensemble practice, and also to studies with Moskovsky. This post was really significant as far as the quartet's future and development were concerned, as he trained us to think about the music we were playing and taught us the art of rehearsing. He was a great inspiration and we really began to get inside the string quartet repertoire.

The fact that we were a resident quartet gave us some stability, and allowed us to rehearse and perform regularly, which enabled us to launch ourselves as a professional ensemble. However, all our concerts outside the university were promoted by ourselves. For our Wigmore Hall début, we invited various agencies to the concert, and one of them took us on. Also pivotal to our success was a BBC audition which resulted in the quartet recording some concerts for broadcast on Radio 3.

From time to time, you have musical arguments, but in a quartet you always maintain respect for the other members and you don't allow yourself to become musically egocentric: there are always two sides to every story, and there is no single way of playing a phrase.

And so rehearsing in a quartet was democratic to a certain degree – each of us talked about our vision and how we related to the music – whereas in an orchestra there is very little that you're allowed to say:

you have to put yourself in the collective and become part of a larger team. When I switched to being a symphonic player, I had to make sure I was in the same part of the bow as everyone else; I had to count the bars' rest, and keep my ears and eyes open. I was used to having a degree of freedom, and to being able to do my own thing within certain parameters; thus in a way I had to be more spontaneous when I was playing in the orchestra. There was a big change for me mentally as well. I went from playing repertoire that I knew inside out – understanding what the composer wanted to say – to playing music that I hadn't experienced before, although I attempted to tackle symphonic music with a chamber musician's mind, searching deeper and trying to see behind the music.

Playing in a quartet for so many years can make you very insular since you are continually with the same people, on stage, in rehearsal and even travelling to concerts in the same car; so that the social life of an orchestra can be a refreshing and welcome change.

The job I have now combines both threads of my career since I organize the orchestral placements within the department as well as coaching students in solo and chamber music.

Our string department currently has a total of two hundred and one students. Quite a few of those will get into orchestral playing, although very few of them will become professional chamber musicians.

We prepare students as much as possible for the profession, but at the same time teach them how to cope with life, encouraging them to be organized, making sure they turn up on time and introducing them to problem-solving. They are also taught how to present and introduce themselves on the platform; and so if a musical career doesn't work out for them, they will have a head start over people who have gone to university and undertaken academic degrees. Companies will pull their CV out of a pile and look at it, because they are experienced performers, and when they go for an interview, they will have a lot more presence than others.

Roger Bigley

Strike Up the Band

There are an infinite number of possible openings for talented and innovative musicians. I know of freelancers who have combined forces and successfully offered educational programmes to schools, and of others who have teamed up with actors and put on their own shows for children. How do you get things like this off the ground and find organizations to hire you?

Tim Williams set up a modern-music group called Psappha.

They now perform all over the world, and have had much music written for them.

Psappha is a contemporary music group that I formed in 1991. It has a core of six players and is incredibly versatile. Depending on the repertoire, we have anything from a solo player on stage to our full complement of thirty musicians.

I have always been very interested in contemporary music, and I performed a lot of new music when I was at college; but I never thought of running a group until I left. I realized that there wasn't a new music ensemble in the North-West, and so I asked some college friends if they would be interested, hired the concert hall at the Royal Northern College of Music, financed it all myself and put on our first concert. It went very well, and we received a good review in the *Guardian*. I then went to the North-West Arts board to try and get some funding, but they refused us and said the group would probably fold within a year or two. Undaunted by this, I looked for contacts in the *British and International Music Yearbook* for engagements, and continued to put on concerts. Eventually, after about three years, we were awarded project-funding from North-West Arts; and three years after that they turned us into an Annually Funded Organization, which means that I have to fill in hundreds of forms. But we do receive regular money. I set Psappha up as a limited company in 1997, and got charitable status for it in 1998.

Even with all the money coming in, I still had to finance the group out of my own pocket for the first five years because the grants we received together with the income that was generated from engagements didn't cover all the costs.

To illustrate how expensive such a music group can be, we recently co-commissioned and co-produced a new music-theatre work by Peter Maxwell Davies called *Mr Emmet Takes a Walk*. We performed it eighteen times and the cost of originating the work, paying ten musicians, three opera singers, three production staff, and a director, designer and lighting engineer, along with transportation to venues ranging from the Orkneys to Paris, came to well over £200,000.

The administrative skills you need to run such an organization don't usually go hand in hand with being a musician, and so I had to learn everything as I went along. When I wanted to know about something, I would track down a book and read about it. For example, when I needed to set up a website for the group, I went on tour with an orchestra in my role as a freelance percussionist and read up about websites on the long coach journeys. When I came home, I set up: *www.psappha.com*.

I play in the group in spite of the fact that I am the manager. I do the books, arrange the concerts, organize tours, get work permits; and it is terribly time-consuming. But I am very pleased with the way the group has developed in the twelve years it has existed. We were awarded the Swatch City Life Award for the Best Concert Series and Education Work in 1995, and the *Manchester Evening News* Award for Opera in 2000, and we have been nominated for the Royal Philharmonic Society Ensemble Award for the last five years. We have never made a loss and our turnover went up from zero in 1991 to over £350,000 in 2000.

I have recently become the artistic director of the Lancaster International Concert Series at the university, which means that I programme the concerts and devise the education programme as well as raising the money for it. I enjoy the variety of what I do; I still freelance with orchestras; and I am also a micro-light flying instructor at weekends! I like to have many strings to my bow: I couldn't just do one job.

I always wanted to be my own boss rather than an employee as I very quickly became bored of waiting for the phone to ring. In the orchestral scene, a lot depends on your relationship with the fixer. Playing in different sections requires you to be what somebody else wants you to be rather than yourself. I did go for jobs in orchestras for a while and I wasn't succeeding. I hope that it was my personality they didn't like rather than my playing. I also decided that I wanted there to be more to life than just playing the triangle here and there. With hindsight, I'm glad I didn't get any of the jobs since I think I'm not an ideal person for a full-time position. When an orchestra offers me freelance work now, I have a choice; and when I accept it, I really enjoy it.

Tim Williams

Original Instruments

I studied in the same class as Rachel Brown. She is a unique talent. She is equally gifted on both modern and original instruments.

> Although I have a deep love of the colour of early instruments, I feel that it is extremely important to play early music on modern instruments. It is really alarming how many modern instrumentalists play almost no baroque music for fear of 'getting it wrong'. For flautists this means that they are not even touching some of the best repertoire. There is a huge amount of good quality solo and chamber music, which so many modern players don't even know exists.
>
> As a child, I started on the recorder and I had a lovely private teacher, Chris Nichols, who wasn't a recorder player but he was a fantastic musician. When I was eleven, I went to the Royal College of Music Junior Department as a flautist. At that point, I just wanted to play the flute, but they were keen to build a recorder department there;

so, one way or another, I was drafted into a recorder ensemble and pre-vailed upon to have recorder lessons, too. We played consort music every week and I loved it. At the Junior Department my recorder teacher, Ross Winters, introduced me to all sorts of articulation and ornamentation along with improvisation. The fact that every time you played something it could be different, I found absolutely fascinating. He was very keen for me to try the baroque flute, but the first few times I heard one I really didn't like it at all, and I had no intention of play-ing one. I then heard Barthold Kuijken on the radio and it stopped me in my tracks. He was playing some Rameau, and it was quite different from anything I had heard before. As with any instrument, when you hear it played well, you will be moved, and when it is not played well, it won't affect you in the same way. I started playing the baroque flute as a subsidiary study and began to understand more of the problems surrounding the instrument, and therefore came to have a more sym-pathetic attitude when hearing one being played, and to admire many qualities in people whose playing I had not understood at first.

At college (as a modern-flute player) my only ambition was to play my flute in the way that I had dreamt of. I had no idea how to earn a living, or how to prepare for an orchestral position. I had a marvellous grounding with my modern teacher, Trevor Wye, studying the solo repertoire and performing the Ibert and Nielsen concertos. They were invaluable opportunities: standing in front of a large orchestra, play-ing complex scores, and being stretched emotionally and technically in a way that simply studying a baroque instrument would not have achieved. In subsequent years, performing and recording phenomenally virtuoso concertos by C.P.E. Bach and playing Beethoven, Schubert, Mendelssohn, Dvořák and Brahms on instruments of the period, I have been so thankful for Trevor's tough but thorough training on the mod-ern instrument which has stood me in very good stead, although stylistically rather different. I would certainly do the same thing again.

Whilst still at the Royal Northern College of Music, I started be-ing offered some professional concerts. My baroque teacher, Lisa Beznosiuk, began drafting me into all sorts of work, which was a real privilege. Over the first few years, I did a fair amount of second play-ing to her – watching the conductor with one eye whilst observing every fingering and nuance in her playing with the other, just as an apprentice would do.

I was lucky that at the time there weren't many people in my field, and I was soon asked to take up the classical (i.e. eight-keyed) flute and later nineteenth century instruments, often with radically different fingering systems. Essentially, I was thrown in at the deep end and had to learn to swim – fast! Learning in public was very stressful.

My first regular job was actually on modern flute with Kent Opera, a touring company with an outstanding orchestra, where I made many treasured musical friends. I revelled in the passionate nineteenth and twentieth century repertoire, but above all the Mozart operas, which have such glorious orchestral parts. I developed a deep appreciation for singers whose words are clear and whose delivery is full of character and colour. My opera training had a profound influence on my playing. Sadly, Kent Opera lost its Arts Council Grant at the point when I began to be asked to do more solo baroque and classical playing. You do get typecast as an original instrumentalist, and I regret not playing the modern flute as much as I would like now; but that may change.

I love the modern flute, and for me it was never a question of believing that music had to be played on original instruments. On the contrary, a lot can be done just as successfully on modern instruments, and I only wish that more modern players played the repertoire and explored the customs of articulation and ornamentation, the rhetoric and the dance styles [see 'Style' in the *Performing Philosophies* chapter (page 47)]. It is sad to think that so many people haven't played the Telemann Paris Quartets, the *Musical Offering* by J.S. Bach, or trio sonatas by C.P.E. Bach, Leclair, Couperin and Marais, all masterpieces which they are missing out on.

Rachel Brown

Management or Administration

The management of a symphony orchestra will seem an obvious choice for some people, either because performing is too stressful for them or because the required standard is unattainable. Or perhaps they may consider this alternative after a successful performing career. In the *Mechanics of the Orchestra* chapter, we found out that most of our seventeen office staff were ex-musicians or had music degrees. How did they make their first step into the management world? I asked our fixer, Helena Miles, to take us through her ascent from college to the orchestral office.

I am a 'cellist but I majored in composition at Bath College of Further Education. I originally wanted to be a teacher. However, I spent one week in schools and decided that that definitely wasn't for me. I stayed on at Bath doing a BA in music, which was a great 'all-round' course. I knew that I wanted to be in music but I didn't want to perform. I am not a performer and never will be. At college, I had organized a lot of concerts which I really enjoyed doing, and so I decided that Arts Administration and Management was the direction to go in. I had musical knowledge but not the secretarial skills required, so I went off and did a one-year course to get a higher diploma in Administrative Procedures. Anyone thinking of following this sort of career must realize that it helps to have computer skills, to know how offices work, and to get as much experience of organizing concerts as possible. The problem after that is getting a job in Arts Administration because there are so many music graduates who want jobs. My first job was Assistant Orchestra Manager at Trinity College of Music and there were 182 applicants.

Helena Miles

Music Critic

Music critics have had some bad press over the years ...

'They ply their saws, and timber and proud oaks
are reduced to sawdust.'
Robert Schumann, 1810–56

Why are some musicians attracted into this profession? What are the essential attributes needed for fulfilling such a calling? Furthermore, what is the purpose of writing a critique? Are they aiming to attract an audience or to educate one? I put forward these questions to pianist, scholar and music critic of the *Daily Telegraph*, David Fanning.

There are two sides to becoming a music critic. First, there is the predisposition: the wanting to do it, getting a buzz from talking about concerts, enjoying swapping opinions, agreeing or disagreeing with the press. Then there is the opportunity: the actual means of becoming one.

As a critic, you need to articulate the experience that you've had. For me, that got sharpened up not just by concert going, but by late-night piano classes held at the Royal Northern College of Music by my teacher, Sulamita Aronovsky. She brought with her the Russian way of getting her entire class together. Every week or so, from about eight in the evening to midnight, we played for one another and criticized. I learned more from that than from any other experience. We might suggest something about a passage that wasn't going quite right, really take it apart and then put it together again so that the phrase would blossom.

As a student, I wrote programme notes for my own concerts, and a couple of people seemed to notice that I did that reasonably well. Gerald Larner, the music critic from the *Guardian*, had been looking for an assistant for several years and it was Aronovsky who said, 'Try

Fanning out!' I was a postgraduate at the time and I did a couple of 'crits' on a trial basis. Afterwards, we discussed them, and that was it. For the first ten years or so, the job was quite fraught: you would go to the concert and phone the review in by 10.30 that same night. If it was not copied and on the editor's desk by 11 p.m. it wouldn't get printed. There was very little time for reflection; you would have to write it in long-hand and find a phone. There were always problems with the copy-taker. It was a great training but inevitably things would turn out a bit sloppy. For instance, once I was complimenting Sir Edward Downes, remarking on the 'X factor' in his performance, and it came out as the 'ex-actor'. These days, the paper is 'put to bed' much earlier, and so now I don't have to email it in until 11 a.m. the next morning.

I don't sit in concerts turning pages of the score, although I will check if something seems odd. When I get home, I'll sit in front of the computer for about an hour (or an hour and a half, if it's a struggle) and type out a 400-word review – the basic slot for the *Telegraph*. Then I print it out, because you always see it differently in hard-copy form – you're more objective reading it that way. In the morning, if I have time before work, I spend fifteen minutes tidying things up a little, email it to the paper and then pray.

I get two complimentary tickets for every concert that I review, and receive £120 for submitting the piece, although not all the articles get published: the papers tend to ask for more copy than they have room for, as they can't afford to have blank space. So occasionally a concert review is considered dispensable.

Any criticism is a balance between having something interesting to say about a programme and something about the performance. A critic needs to develop the vocabulary to be able to say that something is lousy or fantastic without using those words, and in general it's easier to write 'knocking copy'. I don't think that's because I'm nasty; it's just that the English language is so rich for expressing scorn, whereas there aren't too many ways of saying: 'the orchestra reached its usual high standard and as ever was committed and professional'!

I write my criticisms primarily for someone who didn't get to the concert but is really interested to know what's hot and in what terms things are being discussed. I also write for the audience to compare their impressions; very much in third place, I write for the musicians themselves.

David Fanning

At this point in the interview, I made the following comment:

'A musicologist is a man who can read music but can't hear it.'
Sir Thomas Beecham, conductor, 1879–1961

The ideal musician should be able to think as well as play. I wouldn't have the nerve to sit down and write a negative criticism if I couldn't, in principle, go along and say: 'This is what I mean; that's what I'm on about', and then demonstrate it – on the piano. I also wouldn't have the nerve unless I had been 'up there', under that sort of pressure: I know all the things that can go wrong, all the things that are not really under your control because you are obeying someone else's orders, whom you may or may not respect.

David Fanning

Epilogue

'Dust as we are, the immortal spirit grows,
like harmony in music.'
William Wordsworth, 1770–1850

In Bernard Shore's book *The Orchestra Speaks*, the first few pages describe the atmosphere on stage at the Queen's Hall moments before a concert. The year is 1938, and with the exception of the boiled shirts it could have been yesterday. Some violinists are giving a last-minute look at an awkward passage, and checking that they have the correct bowing marked in from the front desk, while the violas are shuffling their chairs around, claiming they have inadequate room. The first clarinettist is looking despairingly over a box full of reeds laid out in front of him, none of which seem to work. He is lent one by his second player, and the concert starts.

Today, as in 1938, there are many colourful characters in the profession, and I think that orchestral life would make an ideal setting for a soap opera. In fact, 'fictitious' books have already been written on the subject that are not that fictitious at all. In a large symphony orchestra, you have ninety intelligent, emotional, expressive people all sitting in close proximity. In my orchestra alone, we have jugglers and writers, artists, photographers, astronomers, exceptional soloists, political animals, lovers, ex-lovers and many, many more. A clarinettist who sat behind me for fifteen years was one of the funniest men alive, and would make you crease up every time he opened his mouth. On tours, if you sat too close to him on the bus, you would find that your diaphragm was unusable by the time you got to the next venue. When you weave such dynamics together and place so many diverse personalities in one room, it is no wonder that there will be high-octane passion when you hear them perform the world's most magnificent music.

All musicians have their own stories to tell, like the clarinettist, just mentioned, who got up in the middle of the night to relieve himself in a Brazilian hotel. Opening the wrong door in the dark, he found himself completely naked in the hotel corridor as his bedroom door locked itself behind him. Thinking quickly, he rushed to the roof-top fitness centre and found something to cover up his pride. He was spotted in the hotel lobby with an inflatable paddling-pool wrapped around him, trying to persuade the night-porter to give him a replacement key.

There are endless stories which would make you weep with laughter but, while telling most of them would be fun, I think I'll leave that for another author.

You will have gathered by now that being a professional orchestral musician is an extraordinarily pressurized though fascinating career. I myself love the challenge and I can't imagine doing anything else. At its best, playing music with sensitive and talented people can be the most breathtaking and enlightening experience you can have. I wish you the best of luck in attaining your goals.

Here are two final anecdotes, to pass on to you the most touching comments I have received as player and teacher. They were not about technical excellence nor were they about a particularly rousing or noble rendering of a work. Each was probably made without any idea of the effect that it might have on me. The first was after an orchestral concert when a guest player leant over my shoulder and said: 'You don't play as if you have been in the profession for twenty years: you still sound fresh!' The other comment came after a class I had taken in Greece. There had been a long day of teaching and a recital, and I was hailing a taxi to the airport when one of the students ran up to me and cried out: 'You opened my eyes.'

> 'Melody is the golden thread running through
> the maze of tones by which the ear is guided
> and the heart reached.'
> Anonymous

Play well and enjoy your musical life.

Index

accent, 48, 143

accompanist, 46, 75, 79, 89

accompany, 46, 68, 76–7, 89, 92, 94, 154, 202; unaccompanied, 76

acoustic(s), 15, 32, 75–6, 109, 129, 144, 157–8, 174, 182, 200

Addinall, Patrick, 7, 39, 95, 147, 197, 199, 214, 217

administration, 187, 220, 223, 226–7

Alcantara, Pedro de, 10, 113

alcohol, 84, 127, 211

anger, 21, 74

Aristotle, 14

articulation, 5, 27, 48, 65, 72, 85–6, 93–5, 118, 144, 156, 167, 181, 210, 215, 225–6

auditions: advice auditions, 19; audition nerves, 72–8; audition panel, 59–62; extra-work auditions, 62, 79, 84, 205, 208; music-college auditions, 36, 40, 47; music-school auditions, 28–9; orchestral auditions, 4–5, 41–2, 45, 52–84, 88, 128, 131, 156, 187, 205, 210; pre-audition, 80–1; post-audition, 81–2; rumours in auditions, 78; screened auditions, 60; youth-orchestra auditions, 28

Augustine, St, v

awareness, 85–6, 111

Banai, Margalit, 10, 138–9

Barbirolli, Sir John, 155

bar-lines, 48–9

beating: conductor's, 140, 142–55, 201, 203

beats: sound-wave interference, 168–70, 174–8, 182

Beecham, Sir Thomas, 145, 182, 228

Beethoven, Ludwig van, 136–7, 199, 209, 225

Berlioz, Hector, 139, 150, 199

beta-blocker, 125–6

Bigley, Roger, 7, 39, 220–2

Bizet, Georges, 185

blending, 28, 53, 65–7, 85, 87, 89–91, 94, 158, 202, 210

booked: being, 88, 205–8; double-booking, 189, 207

bowings, 153, 195–6, 230

Bradbury, John, 7, 37–8, 197, 200, 202

breathing, 45, 129, 195, 213, 219

British and International Music Yearbook, 223

Brown, Rachel, 7–8, 173, 224–6

Brymer, Jack, 156

Bülow, Hans von, 115

bumping, 195, 209

'cello strings, 194

cents, 169–75

chamber music, 4, 37, 220–2, 224

Chasey, Robert, 8, 63, 86, 151, 156, 196, 212

Chatterton, Tim, 8, 200–1

Chetham's School of Music, 9, 30–1

cochlea, 109, 157, 180

colours, 28, 32, 65, 85, 90–3, 117, 158–66, 200

comma, 169–74; diatonic, 169, 171; syntonic, 171

Comment Sheet, 81–2

communication: through conducting, 151; through playing, 5, 42, 120

counting, 68, 133–42, 222

Coward, Noël, 112

critic, music, 9, 21, 59, 119, 136, 227–9

233